ISSUES THAT CONCERN YOU

Dieting

Arthur Gillard, *Book Editor*

GREENHAVEN PRESS
A part of Gale, Cengage Learning

GALE
CENGAGE Learning·

Detroit • New York • San Francisco • New Haven, Conn • Waterville, Maine • London

Elizabeth Des Chenes, *Director, Content Strategy*
Cynthia Sanner, *Publisher*
Douglas Dentino, *Manager, New Product*

LIBRARY OF CONGRESS CATALOGING-IN-PUBLICATION DATA

Dieting / Arthur Gillard, book editor.
  pages cm. -- (Issues that concern you)
 Summary: "Issues That Concern You: Dieting: This series provides readers with information on topics of current interest. Focusing on important social issues, each anthology examines its subject in a variety of ways, from personal accounts to factual articles"-- Provided by publisher.
 Includes bibliographical references and index.
 ISBN 978-0-7377-6938-8 (hardback)
 1. Nutrition. 2. Diet. 3. Food habits. I. Gillard, Arthur, editor of compilation.
 RA784.D55 2014
 613.2--dc23
                                                              2013049046

Printed in the United States of America
1 2 3 4 5 6 7 18 17 16 15 14

CONTENTS

For most of human history, food was in short supply, and obesity was not a problem for the vast majority of people—whose main challenge was getting enough food to survive. In the modern world, however, overconsumption has in general become more of a problem than scarcity, at least in developed parts of the world such as the United States. As Peter Kaminsky, author of *Culinary Intelligence: The Art of Eating Healthy (and Really Well)* notes, "There are almost a billion and a half overweight people in the world, nearly twice as many as the underweight figure of eight hundred million."[1] The 2012 report *Weight in America: Obesity, Eating Disorders, and Other Health Risks* reported that as of 2010, 32 percent of all US children were obese or overweight. According to the Centers for Disease Control and Prevention (CDC), in 2009, 33 percent of US adults were overweight, and 34 percent were obese (extremely overweight). Expanding waistlines in America have brought with them a national obsession with dieting and weight reduction. A 2012 survey by the International Food Information Council Foundation (IFIC) reported that 55 percent of the US population is attempting to lose weight.

There are a number of theories as to what causes excessive weight gain. The "energy balance" or "calories-in/calories-out" theory is one of the most popular; it considers weight gain to be a simple matter of physics: If someone consumes more calories (a measure of the amount of energy in food) than one expends through exercise, weight gain will be the result. Others maintain that weight gain is modulated by hormones in the body; for example, insulin is primarily responsible for weight gain because it determines how much of the food eaten is converted to fat. The theory of weight gain determines what is considered the appropriate response to return weight to a healthy balance. The energy balance framework implies that reducing weight is a simple matter of consuming fewer calories or burning more calories by exercising more. On the other hand, if one believes that insulin imbalance is the culprit, then reducing the amount of simple carbohydrates (such as bread, pasta, and sugar) is the way to get back to a healthy weight.

Newer theories suggest that environmental influences that disrupt normal metabolism—the chemical processes that take place in cells and organisms to maintain life—are largely to blame for the pervasive weight gain in the United States and other industrialized countries. For example, some research suggests that excessive use of antibiotics may disrupt the complex ecosystem of microorganisms that live in the digestive tract, leading to weight gain. Interestingly, farm animals fed low doses of antibiotics gain weight. In an experiment by New York University microbiologists published in *Nature* in 2012, lab mice given low doses of antibiotics saw an increase in body fat of 15 percent, and the composition of bacteria in their intestinal tract was much different than that in mice who were not fed antibiotics.

Other research raises questions about a class of chemicals called endocrine disruptors, which act on the body in a similar way to hormones, enhancing or suppressing normal hormonal responses. Such chemicals, including phthalates, polychlorinated biphenyls (PCBs), and bisphenol A, are widely used in consumer products and are pervasive in the environment. Studies have linked endocrine disrupters to impaired immune functioning, early puberty, and various diseases, including cancer—and more recent research suggests that they might be disrupting normal metabolism and causing obesity. Laura Fraser, in a 2011 article for the website Grist, points out that, intriguingly,

> studies . . . show that animals that live in human environments get fatter just by virtue of being around people. Researchers at the University of Alabama recently found that chimpanzees, macaques [a type of monkey], mice, rats, dogs, cats, and other species that lived in proximity to humans got fatter than animals that didn't live in an industrialized environment—even when their lab chow and exercise was highly controlled. The authors suggested that endocrine disruptors were one likely culprit in this cross-species obesity epidemic.[2]

In America there is a growing national obsession with dieting. The International Food Information Council Foundation reports that 55 percent of the US population is attempting to lose weight.

Some call into question the whole premise of dieting to lose or maintain weight. Advocates of "fat acceptance" or "health at any size" say the emphasis on maintaining a particular weight is harmful to people who naturally have larger bodies, or who have tried and failed to lose weight. They point out that dieting can have deleterious effects on health and can lead to eating disorders, especially in young people. They point to studies suggesting that for most people dieting is unsuccessful and may even—especially in the case of repeated or extreme dieting—lead to increased weight in the long run. Of particular concern is "fat shaming" and discrimination against overweight people. In the opinion of Rockefeller University obesity researcher Jeffrey Friedman, "Obese people get a level of abuse now that could not even be considered with any other group."[3] Yale University psychologist Rebecca Puhl warns that "stigma is not an effective motivator. Whether children or adults, if they are teased or stigmatized, they're much more likely to engage in unhealthy eating and avoidance of physical activity."[4] Rather than emphasizing the pursuit of thinness per se, critics of the "war on obesity" suggest it would be better to accept that people have a variety of body types and sizes, and encourage good nutrition and exercise for everyone.

The study of diet and obesity is complex and controversial, and there is much yet to be discovered. In all likelihood overweight and obesity result from a complex interaction of many factors. Some of those factors may need to be addressed at a society-wide or environmental level, while others are more amenable to individual control. Despite the diverse range of opinions on the topic, most people would agree that exercise and good nutrition are healthy options for all.

The authors in this anthology offer a variety of perspectives on dieting. In addition, the volume contains several appendixes to help the reader to further understand and explore the topic, including a thorough bibliography and a list of organizations to contact for further information. The appendix titled "What You Should Know About Dieting" offers facts about the subject. The appendix "What You Should Do About Dieting" offers advice for young people who are concerned with this issue. With all these features, *Issues That Concern You: Dieting* provides an excellent resource for everyone interested in this increasingly charged topic.

Notes
1. Peter Kaminsky, *Culinary Intelligence: The Art of Eating Healthy (and Really Well)*. New York: Knopf, 2012, p. 35.

2. Laura Fraser. "Is Your Shampoo Making You Fat?," Grist, June 28, 2011. http://grist.org/living/2011-06-28-is-your-shampoo -making-you-fat/.

3. Gina Kolata, *Rethinking Thin: The New Science of Weight Loss— and the Myths and Realities of Dieting.* New York: Farrar, Straus, and Giroux, 2007, p. 18.

4. David Crary, "Skeptics Warn of Stigma amid 'War on Obesity,'" Association for Size Diversity and Health, May 1, 2011. www .sizediversityandhealth.org/content.asp?id=34&articleID=164.

ONE

An Overview of Dieting

David Helwig and Teresa G. Odle

David Helwig and Teresa G. Odle have authored numerous articles for *The Gale Encyclopedia of Medicine* and other medical encyclopedias. In the following viewpoint Helwig and Odle note that people adopt special diets for a variety of reasons, such as to prevent disease, increase health, lose weight, or for ethical reasons. According to the authors, those who are overweight can experience improved health through sensible dieting; however, there are dangers and pitfalls in commonly practiced diets, particularly in the case of fad diets. For example, "yo-yo dieting," in which a cycle of weight loss/regain occurs, can cause the metabolism to slow down, making future weight reduction more difficult. Yo-yo dieting also increases the risk of developing an eating disorder. The authors suggest that a long-term approach that involves healthy lifestyle changes is a better approach than quick-fix diets that promise big weight loss in a short period of time.

Humans may alter their usual eating habits for many reasons, including weight loss, disease prevention or treatment, removing toxins from the body, or to achieve a general improvement in physical and mental health. Others adopt special diets

David Helwig and Teresa G. Odle, "Diets," *The Gale Encyclopedia of Medicine*, ed. Laurie J. Fundukian, vol. 2, 2011. From, Gale Encyclopedia of Medicine V2, 4E. Copyright © 2011 Cengage Learning.

for religious reasons. In the case of some vegetarians and vegans, dietary changes are made out of ethical concerns for the rights of animals.

People who are moderately to severely overweight can derive substantial health benefits from a weight-loss diet. A weight reduction of just 10–20 pounds can result in reduced cholesterol levels and lower blood pressure. Weight-related health problems include heart disease, diabetes, high blood pressure, and high levels of blood sugar and cholesterol.

In individuals who are not overweight, dietary changes also may be useful in the prevention or treatment of a range of ailments including acquired immune deficiency syndrome (AIDS), cancer, osteoporosis, inflammatory bowel syndrome, chronic pulmonary disease, renal disease, Parkinson's disease, seizure disorders, and food allergies and intolerances.

Origins of Dieting

The practice of altering diet for special reasons has existed since antiquity. For example, Judaism has included numerous dietary restrictions for thousands of years. One ancient Jewish sect, the Essenes, is said to have developed a primitive detoxification diet aimed at preparing the bodies, minds, and spirits of its members for the coming of a "messiah" who would deliver them from their Roman captors. Preventive and therapeutic diets became popular during the late twentieth century. Books promoting the latest dietary plan continue to make the bestseller lists, although not all of the information given is considered authoritative.

The idea of a healthful diet is to provide all of the calories and nutrients needed by the body for optimal performance, at the same time ensuring that neither nutritional deficiencies nor excesses occur. Diet plans that claim to accomplish those objectives are so numerous they are virtually uncountable. These diets employ a variety of approaches, including the following:

- *Fixed-menu*: Offers little choice to the dieter. Specifies exactly which foods will be consumed. Easy to follow, but may be considered boring to some dieters.

- *Formula*: Replaces some or all meals with a nutritionally balanced liquid formula or powder.
- *Exchange-type*: Allows the dieter to choose between selected foods from each food group.
- *Flexible*: Doesn't concern itself with the overall diet, simply with one aspect, such as fat or energy.

Diets also may be classified according to the types of foods they allow. For example, an omnivorous diet consists of both animal and plant foods, whereas a lacto-ovo-vegetarian diet permits no animal flesh, but includes eggs, milk, and other dairy products. A vegan diet is a stricter form of vegetarianism in which eggs, cheese, and other milk products are prohibited.

A third way of classifying diets is according to their purpose: religious, weight-loss, detoxification, lifestyle-related, or aimed at prevention or treatment of a specific disease.

Precautions

Dieters should be cautious about plans that severely restrict the size of food portions, or that eliminate entire food groups from the diet. It is highly probable that they will become discouraged and drop out of such programs. The best diet is one that can be maintained indefinitely without ill effects, that offers sufficient variety and balance to provide everything needed for good health, and that is considerate of personal food preferences. Many controversies have arisen in the past over the benefits and risks of high-protein, low carbohydrate diets such as the Atkins diet. Most physician groups and health organizations have spoken out negatively against the program. In 2003, these statements were largely supported. Though clinical trials showed that these types of diets worked in lowering weight without raising cholesterol for the short-term, many of the participants gained a percentage of the weight back after only one year. A physician group also spoke out about high protein diets' dangers for people with decreased kidney function and the risk of bone loss due to decreased calcium intake.

Low-fat diets are not recommended for children under the age of two. Young children need extra fat to maintain their active,

The authors suggest that a long-term approach that involves healthy lifestyle changes and healthful foods is a better approach than quick-fix diets that promise big weight loss in a short period of time.

growing bodies. Fat intake may be gradually reduced between the ages of two and five, after which it should be limited to a maximum of 30% of total calories through adulthood. Saturated fat should be restricted to no more than 10% of total calories.

Weight-loss dieters should be wary of the "yo-yo" effect that occurs when numerous attempts are made to reduce weight using high-risk, quick-fix diets. This continued "cycling" between weight loss and weight gain can slow the basal metabolic rate and can sometimes lead to eating disorders. The dieter may become discouraged and frustrated by this success/failure cycle. The end result of yo-yo dieting is that it becomes more difficult to maintain a healthy weight.

US Department of Agriculture MyPyramid Food Recommendations

Daily caloric intake	1,000	1,200	1,400	1,600	1,800	2,000
Fruits	1 cup	1 cup	1.5 cups	1.5 cups	1.5 cups	2 cups
Vegetables	1 cup	1.5 cup	1.5 cups	2 cups	2.5 cups	2.5 cups
Grains	3 oz-eq	4 oz-eq	5 oz-eq	5 oz-eq	6 oz-eq	6 oz-eq
Meat and beans	2 oz-eq	3 oz-eq	4 oz-eq	5 oz-eq	5 oz-eq	5.5 oz-eq
Milk	2 cups	2 cups	2 cups	3 cups	3 cups	3 cups
Oils	3 tsp	4 tsp	4 tsp	5 tsp	5 tsp	6 tsp
Discretionary calorie allowance	165	171	171	132	195	267

Daily caloric intake	2,200	2,400	2,600	2,800	3,000	3,200
Fruits	2 cups	2 cups	2 cups	2.5 cups	2.5 cups	2.5 cups
Vegetables	3 cups	3 cups	3.5 cups	3.5 cups	4 cups	4 cups
Grains	7 oz-eq	8 oz-eq	9 oz-eq	10 oz-eq	10 oz-eq	10 oz-eq
Meat and beans	6 oz-eq	6.5 oz-eq	6.5 oz-eq	7 oz-eq	7 oz-eq	7 oz-eq
Milk	3 cups	3 cups	3 cups	3 cups	3 cups	3 cups
Oils	6 tsp	7 tsp	8 tsp	8 tsp	10 tsp	11 tsp
Discretionary calorie allowance	290	362	410	426	512	648

Taken from: US Department of Agriculture, Center for Nutrition Policy and Promotion. David Helwig and Teresa G. Odle. "Diets." *The Gale Encyclopedia of Medicine*. Ed. Laurie J. Fundukian. 4th ed., vol. 2. Detroit: Gale, 2011. Gale Virtual Reference Library.

Fad Diets

Caution also should be exercised about weight loss diets that require continued purchases of special prepackaged foods. Not only do these tend to be costly and over-processed, they also may prevent dieters from learning the food-selection and preparation skills essential to maintenance of weight loss. Further, dieters should consider whether they want to carry these special foods to work, restaurants, or homes of friends.

Concern has been expressed about weight-loss diet plans that do not include exercise, considered essential to long-term weight management. Some diets and supplements may be inadvisable for patients with special conditions or situations. In fact, use of the weight loss supplement ephedra was found to cause serious conditions such as heart attack and stroke. In 2003, the U.S. Food and Drug Administration (FDA) was considering controlling or banning the supplement. [The FDA banned ephedra-containing supplements in 2004.] In short, most physician organizations see fad diets as distracting from learning how to achieve weight control over the long term through healthy lifestyle changes such as eating smaller, more balanced meals and exercising regularly.

Certain fad diets purporting to be official diets of groups such as the American Heart Association and the Mayo Clinic are in no way endorsed by those institutions. People thinking of starting such a diet should check with the institution to ensure its name has not been misappropriated by an unscrupulous practitioner.

A wide range of side effects (some quite serious) can result from special diets, especially those that are nutritionally unbalanced. Further problems can arise if the dieter is taking high doses of dietary supplements. Food is essential to life, and improper nutrition can result in serious illness or death.

It is agreed among traditional and complementary practitioners that many patients could substantially benefit from improved eating habits. Specialized diets have proved effective against a wide variety of conditions and diseases. However, dozens of unproved but widely publicized fad diets emerge each year, prompting widespread concerns about their usefulness, cost to the consumer, and their safety.

TWO

Dieting for Weight Loss Is Completely Ineffective

Megan McArdle

> Megan McArdle is a Washington, D.C.–based blogger and journalist. In the following selection McArdle argues that the history of weight-loss dieting has been one of universal failure. While modest amounts of weight may be lost by some people—usually temporarily—it is virtually never the case, she claims, that those who are overweight enough to cause significant health problems are able to lose enough weight to make a difference. The author cites research in which overweight people were put on extremely restrictive diets and lost large amounts of weight. Although subjects may have resembled someone who had never been overweight, psychologically and metabolically they had many characteristics of people who were starving, and the weight lost always came back. Furthermore, their bodies had changed in such a way that they burned far fewer calories than someone who had never been overweight. McArdle concludes that efforts to lose weight are misguided.

A typical dialogue on diet goes something like this:

Expert: We don't have any known way to make obese people thin except gastric bypass surgery, which has a 2% mortality rate by itself.

Thin person: But I am very thin!

That's about 50% of the conversation in the comments to the [author of *The Obesity Myth*] Paul Campos interview [in the July 29, 2009, *Atlantic Monthly*]. It's about as useful as the following exchange:

Expert: We don't have any known way to make short people tall, except for extreme surgeries and hormone injections.

Megan: But I am 6'2"

Height and Weight

Let's explore the possible rejoinders to this:

1. *Obesity is increasing in the population, so it can't be genetic.*

   Well, average height is also increasing in the population. Does that mean that you could be as tall as me, if you weren't too lazy to grow?

   [Studies of twins and adopted children] show that the overwhelming determinant of your weight is not your willpower; it's your genes. The heritability of weight is between .75 and .85 [i.e., 75–85 percent of weight is influenced by genetics]. The heritability of height is between .9 and .95. And the older you are, the more heritable weight is.

2. *Height doesn't have anything to do with health.*

   Actually, it may. Being taller puts a greater strain on your circulatory, cardiovascular, and musculoskeletal systems. Tall people are prone to all sorts of problems at higher rates, especially in their back[s]. That doesn't make it any more sensible to suggest that we need a public health campaign to help tall people shrink.

The Difficulty of Losing Weight

3. *We don't have any good way to make people shorter, but we do know how to make them lose weight.*

   Actually, this is rubbish: we don't know how to lose weight. Some of the things Paul Campos is saying about obesity are controversial, but this isn't. Every single study which has attempted to make overweight people get thin without very risky surgery has failed completely and utterly. Fewer than 1% of patients ever keep the weight off.

Highly educated people who have managed to get their body weight down 5–10% from where their body naturally wants to be confuse what they are doing with what someone obese enough to cause significant medical problems would need to do, which is get their weight down 50% or more from where their body apparently wants it. They are not the same thing. The amount of weight loss that these sanctimonious slenderizers have achieved has no statistically significant health benefits. Let me repeat: losing twenty pounds will not make you healthier. If you have diabetes and high blood pressure, there is an extremely modest improvement in test results. Unfortunately, it's even harder for diabetics to lose weight than the rest of us.

The Rockefeller Weight-Loss Study

Fat tissue makes people want to eat—it sends out for takeout. And hunger is a signal on par with thirst or pain. You can ignore it, if you have sufficient willpower. But just as most people can't withstand torture (a minority can), most people can't ignore the constant demand from their body for food. [*New York Times* writer] Gina Kolata's *Rethinking Thin* describes it thus:

Every time the result was the same. The weight, so painstakingly lost, came right back. But since this was a research study, the scientists looked at more than just weight loss . . . they measured metabolic changes and psychiatric conditions and body temperature and pulse. And that led them to a surprising conclusion: fat people who lose large amounts of weight may look like someone who was never fat, but they are very different. In fact, by every measurement they seemed like people who were starving.

On every count, the weird, bizarre, almost depraved behavior that Ancel Keys reported when he studied young men who were deliberately starved in his experiment during World

War II was just like what [researcher Jules] Hirsch observed among the formerly obese subjects at Rockefeller University Hospital. Something was driving these people to regain their weight, and it was not a deep-seated desire to be fat.

Their metabolisms, for example, had changed so that they hung onto, clung to, every calorie that was consumed, making it harder for them to stay thin. Before the study began, the fat people had a normal metabolism—the number of calories burned per square inch of body surface was the same as for people who had never been fat. That changed substantially after they lost weight, with fat people burning 24% fewer calories per square meter of surface area than were used by people who were naturally thin.

The Rockefeller subjects also had a psychiatric condition that had been termed "semi-starvation neurosis." Hirsch's patients dreamed about food; they fantasized about food, or breaking their diets. They secreted food in their rooms. They daydreamed about food. And they binged . . . eventually more than fifty people went through the months-long process of living in the hospital and losing weight, and every one of them had the physical and psychiatric symptoms of starvation.

Naturally Thin People Are Not Superior to Overweight People

If when eating a normal 2,000–2,500 calorie diet, you do not spend significant amounts of your day fixating on food—fantasizing about it, binging, hiding it, strategizing how to procure it—you do not have anything interesting to say to someone who is struggling with obesity. You do not have better willpower than they do. You do not "care about myself" more. You are not more "serious about a healthy lifestyle" because you took off the eight pounds you gained at Christmas. You are no more qualified to lecture the obese on how to lose weight than I am qualified to lecture my short friends on how to become tall. You just have a different environmental and genetic legacy than they do. You're not superior. You're just somewhat thinner.

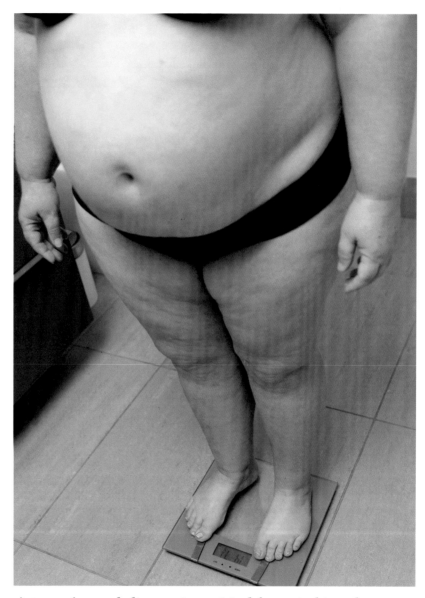

A person's metabolic rate is a critical factor in his or her ability to lose weight.

To put it another way: I have NEVER had a BMI [body mass index] above the normal range. How much more awesome am I than you? 30%? After all, you have to work at it. My willpower is apparently 100% natural.

I fearlessly predict that more than one person will respond with some variation on "there were no fat people in concentration camps/but I *told* you, I totally lost 20 pounds last year by taking up marathon running!" Yes, we could solve America's obesity problem by putting everyone in the country on sawdust bread and cabbage soup. We could also just shoot anyone whose BMI is over 28. Are these good solutions? Because short of that, we don't have much.

4. *Then we need to intervene with the kids, so they don't get fat in the first place.*

Schools have tried this; so far, it's no more successful than adult interventions. You can get a very small effect over the short term, but eventually, the kids start eating again. Yes, school meals are crap. I assure you, they were also crap thirty years ago, and sixty years ago. Yes, P/E [physical education] has been cut in some schools, but there's little evidence that exercising makes you lose weight by itself. Unless you control their access to food completely—and you can't—those kinds of environmental interventions don't work.

Possible Causes of Increased Obesity

5. *So why is America getting fatter, Miss Smartypants?*

Some combination of the following:

1. *Hyperpalatability of food:* the [diet guru] Seth Roberts/ chain restaurant haters hypothesis. The processors have perfected combinations of fat, salt and sugar that addict us, causing us to eventually swell up like a balloon.

   But French restaurants have been doing this for over a century, and for most of that century, thinness has been inversely correlated with poverty. Your body doesn't care whether it gets its fat and sugar from a Ho-Ho or a Chocolate Eclair.

2. *Increasing prevalence of corn in the supply chain:* the [*Omnivore's Dilemma* author] Michael Pollan/Cato [Institute, a Washington, D.C., think tank,] hypothesis. Maybe: corn doesn't seem to be very good for you. But I'm skeptical of monocausal [single-cause] hypotheses.

3. *Calories are getting cheaper*. Self explanatory. In my view, the dominant reason. People eat more calories because they like it, and can afford to.

4. *Animal fat*. Eh, maybe. We sure eat a lot more of it than we used to. But we eat a lot more of everything. And without controlling for socioeconomic status, it's hard to tell whether vegetarians are thinner.

5. *Larger portions*. Special case of "calories are getting cheaper." I think it's less persuasive than many people think. It's true people will eat a great deal at a sitting if you give them a great deal. But if people were so easy to fool, long term, about their caloric intake, we'd all weigh eight zillion pounds.

   As I pointed out elsewhere, a simple error of 50 calories a day—half a slice of Pepperidge Farm All-Natural Whole Wheat Bread—would make us gain five pounds a year apiece. Given inherent calculation error, no one is watching their calories this carefully. Our appetites are doing the work for us. Maybe you eat an extra 2,000 stealth calories at dinner, but you're not so hungry the next day. Conversely, try dining on Macaroni Grill's new 390 calorie scallop salad. Unless you're on a permanent diet, I bet you feel peckish before bed.

6. *We're getting older*. It is normal to gain weight as you age, unless you are in a fairly calorie-deprived environment. An aging demographic will naturally produce a fatter population. This does not account for the growing number of super-obese people with BMIs over 40, even over 50. But it accounts for at least some of the central shift.

7. *We quit smoking*. Smoking makes you quite a lot thinner, particularly after 25. Now that fewer adults smoke, more adults are gaining weight.

Popular-but-Incorrect Ideas on Why Obesity Has Increased

Reasons we aren't getting fat:

1. *We don't know how many calories are in the food we're eating*. I'm pretty sure my great-grandmother didn't either. She still knew that pound cake made you fat, and lettuce didn't.

BMI Visual Graph

Body mass index (BMI) is a standard way of measuring a person's weight in relation to his or her height, used to determine if the person is under- or overweight.

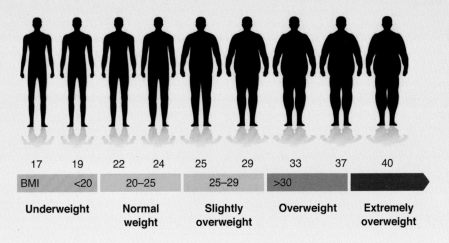

17	19	22	24	25	29	33	37	40

BMI	<20	20–25	25–29	>30	
Underweight	**Normal weight**	**Slightly overweight**	**Overweight**	**Extremely overweight**

Taken from: "BMI Visual Graph." Healthy Weight Forum. www.healthyweightforum.org/eng/calculators/bmi-visual-graph/.

2. *We exercise less.* We haven't gotten noticeably more sedentary in the past decade or so, but the weights keep shooting up. Also, there's no evidence that exercise makes you lose weight—ever discussed dieting with a long distance runner or ballerina?

3. *Poor people don't have access to good groceries.* They had even worse access ten, thirty, fifty years ago. Using starch and cheap sugar as substitutes for vegetables and lean meat is not a recent invention—[social critic and novelist] George Orwell discussed it in the *Road to Wigan Pier.* Frozen vegetables are very good for you, and within the budget of everyone.

4. *We're eating too many empty carbs.* Processed carbs entered—and dominated—the American diet in the second half of the nineteenth century. Working people at the turn of the century ate virtually no meat, little fat, and few vegetables; their diets were mostly beans, white flour, polished rice, pasta, and potatoes,

washed down by sugared coffee or tea. Folks who want to blame the "food pyramid" should read a cookbook from 1950. Grandma didn't need a food pyramid to rely mostly on carbs; carbohydrates were *what she could afford*.

A Universal History of Weight-Loss Failure

There is a really, really deep resistance to the idea that appetite is as powerful a modulator as it appears to be. I can't help but believe that at least part of this is simply that thinness, especially for women, is tightly correlated with socioeconomic status and urban living, and nice upper middle class people who have been on a slight diet for most of their adult lives just cannot believe that a) this isn't making them healthier and b) it isn't making them better people.

But while a lot of what Paul Campos says is controversial, this isn't. You can find the same results yourself by reading any study of weight loss; outside of gastric bypass surgery, no system has ever produced any significant long-term weight loss. *None*. As Paul remarked to me once, "We've run this experiment approximately 220 million times and the result is always the same. Why can't anyone believe it?"

His controversial assertions are about the correlation between weight and health, and the benefits of gastric bypass surgery. I'll leave those for another day. But even if he's entirely wrong about those things, we're still left with the core fact: we have tried, and failed, for more than fifty years, to find a way to make people thinner. Arguably, we should stop. Certainly, we shouldn't count on any cost savings from controlling obesity to fund our future health efforts. It is much more likely than not that obesity will stay the same, or get worse.

THREE

Effective Use of Willpower Facilitates Dieting

Pat Koch

Pat Koch is a certified strength and conditioning specialist and a sports nutritionist with the International Society of Sports Nutrition. In the following viewpoint Koch argues that most people who attempt to lose weight fail because they do not understand the most effective way to use willpower. Willpower is a finite resource, Koch asserts, and if one tries to use it to resist temptations (such as junk food) directly, willpower will become depleted, resulting in poor, impulsive choices. According to the author, restrictive dieting also causes stress, which tends to cause weight gain. Koch suggests that the best way to use willpower is to proactively set up the conditions for a healthy lifestyle—for example, by purchasing healthier foods instead of junk food or by cooking healthy food to bring to work in order to more easily avoid choosing less-healthful alternatives available there.

Willpower is a word of contention in the world of dieting. Many assume a dieter's success to be solely determined by how much willpower he has and go as far as to say that a large contributor to obesity is lack of willpower.

Others believe willpower to be out of one's control, saying that no one inherently has more or less willpower, but that success comes easier to some people who are more willing to change their habits.

Attributing failure solely based on willpower is antiquated and discredits other important factors governing weight loss such as interactions between hunger hormones, brain chemicals, genetics, and the influence of habits.

However, your mentality does affect your ability to lose weight— it directly correlates to how much you can change your eating habits. Managed correctly, willpower can set the stage for successful weight loss. The key is a shift in mindset: willpower isn't best used to resist the daily temptation of cravings and hunger. Its best use is as a powerful force directing improvements of our eating habits.

The Physical Basis of Willpower

A distinct mental and physical process, the physical basis of willpower gives us insight on how to best use willpower for weight loss. Our prefrontal cortex is the part of the brain scientists accredit to helping people prioritize goals, control emotions, and temporarily override wants and needs and is believed to be responsible for self-control.

Willpower, as a function of brain activity, runs on blood glucose (carbs). Continuous acts of self-control deplete blood glucose, which is a limited energy source. When blood glucose is low, failures in self-control become more likely, rendering willpower less effective. Studies confirm that restoring blood glucose to adequate levels typically improves self-control.

All this presents a catch-22: drinking something like a sugary soda to re-up on your willpower seems, and is, counter productive. Not only is willpower easily depleted in restrictive dieters, but unrealistic diets that require a high degree of willpower also cause significant stress. The constant restraint imposed from resisting certain foods or a certain amount of food raises the stress hormone Cortisol. Chronically elevated Cortisol is associated with increases in appetite and weight gain.

In a public opinion poll conducted by the Gallup organization in 2008, most respondents expressed the opinion that eating/lifestyle habits are primarily responsible for people being overweight or obese.

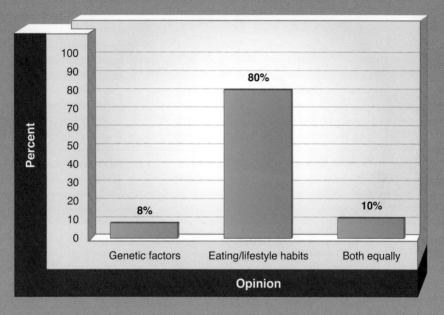

Taken from: Barbara Wexler. "Public Opinion and Action About Diet, Weight, Nutrition, and Physical Activity." *Weight in America: Obesity, Eating Disorders, and Other Health Risks.* Detroit: Gale, 2011.

These two factors may explain why strict dieting often proves unsuccessful. It would appear that the more you need to rely on willpower in your diet the more likely you will fail. While short term it might succeed, over time such restraint erodes. Typically, crash dieters fall back into old habits because the measures they have chosen are not sustainable.

Willpower and Decisions

We use willpower for each and every decision we make. An overabundance of decisions throughout the day leads to mental

The author claims that creating healthful habits and conditions—such as not having junk food in the house and taking a healthful lunch to work instead of eating out—are more effective than simply avoiding temptation.

fatigue. No matter how rational or logical you are, it becomes easier to act impulsively rather than make a thoughtful choice.

Along this line, having an environment that requires you to make many decisions each time you want to eat, can also work against you because you will eventually act impulsively. If you eat out for lunch and dinner every day and don't have your meals planned in advance, chances are you won't make the best choices.

How to Leverage Your Willpower

Finite and exhaustible, dedicate your willpower to making a plan and building momentum with relatively simple changes. You can't lose significant weight in a week, but you can go shopping for healthy food, cook a week's worth of meals, and get rid of the junk food in your house in one day. Over time habits become automatic. Once they don't require decision-making or a high degree of willpower, success will come with less effort and you will be able to take another step that requires a higher degree of willpower.

To will your plan into action, create an environment for success. Use your willpower to concentrate on changing your habits. Do you eat in front of the TV every night? Did you get rid of the junk and stock your kitchen with fruit and veggies? Are you controlling your food by cooking in advance and bringing your lunch to work? Use the following plan to start changing your habits.

Identify six action items you believe will contribute to a healthier you. After you have listed six, rank them from what would be easiest to change all the way down to hardest.

For example:

1. Do not eat in front of the TV. (3 weeks)
2. Cut out calorie laden drinks. Opt for water, teas, etc. (3 weeks)
3. Eat at least 5 servings of fruits and veggies a day (3 weeks)
4. No processed snacks (3 weeks)
5. Limit your alcohol (3 weeks)
6. Pre-cook a coming week's meals (3 weeks)

The idea would be to start on action one and stick with it for three weeks devoting your willpower exclusively to that goal. As you move down the list continue your momentum and attack the next goal for three weeks slowly building until you reach the end. Keep in mind that small changes can add up to big results.

Get Started

By focusing on slowly easing into change it becomes much less stressful to adhere to. Over the course of a couple months you can add in several healthier habits.

It's important to remember that temptation will challenge you. Sometimes your willpower may break, but it isn't a weakness in character, it is a natural tendency to want to indulge when restrained. If you feel too restrained, chances are you might be relying too much on your willpower. Instead, take another look at your habits and make a plan for success!

FOUR

Yo-Yo Dieting Is Healthier than Not Dieting

Ken Tudor

Ken Tudor has graduate training in exercise physiology/ sports nutrition and is the developer of Pet Weight Management, a veterinary practice focused on pet weight loss and management. In the following selection Tudor argues that yo-yo dieting, or cycling repeatedly between weight loss and gain, produces significant positive health benefits. He cites research on mice that found that mice that underwent repeated weight loss/gain were as healthy and lived as long as mice that remained at a low weight; conversely, mice that were kept overweight had shortened lives. Tudor claims that a great deal of research on many different animal species (including humans) shows that measurable signs of good health increase immediately when weight is lost; other research on cats, dogs, and humans shows poor health outcomes associated with ongoing obesity. He concludes that any time spent reducing weight, in people or their pets, positively impacts health.

Here we are again; resolution season. It is that time when we resolve to take extra weight off ourselves and our pets. Most of us, and our pets, will fail miserably at achieving long term results, but may celebrate some short-term victories. And, actually, that may not be as bad as we think.

The yo-yo cycle of weight loss and weight gain is still healthier than no weight loss at all. A recent study in mice showed no life expectancy differences between weight controlled individuals and individuals that experienced repeated weight loss and weight regain cycles.

The Yo-Yo Diet Study

Mice were divided into three feeding programs for their entire lives. One group was fed a low fat diet and maintained at a normal body weight. A second group was fed 4-week cycles of low fat diets and high fat diets and experienced a yo-yo cycle of weight gain and weight loss. The third group was fed a high fat diet and maintained a lifetime overweight status.

A study found that mice that underwent repeated cycles of weight loss and regain were as healthy and lived as long as mice that remained at a low weight, whereas mice that were kept overweight had shortened lives.

The Beneficial Effect of Yo-Yo Dieting in Mice

In an Ohio University study published in 2011, mice fed in a "yo-yo diet" pattern of alternating high-fat and low-fat food lived almost as long as mice fed a low-fat diet for their entire lives, while obese mice kept on a high-fat diet for their entire lives had a significantly shortened life span.

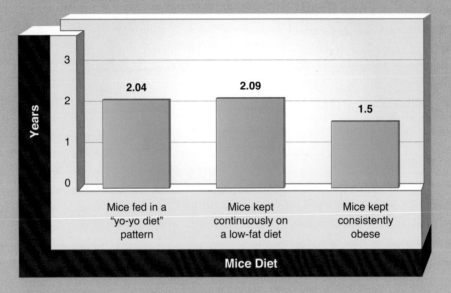

Taken from: "Yo-Yo Dieting vs. Obesity? Dieters May Be Healthier, Live Longer, Study Finds." Ohio University Office of Research, Communications, June 6, 2011. www.ohio.edu/research/communications/yoyodiet.cfm.

The high fat, overweight group had significantly shorter lives. The lifespans for the low fat and cycled groups were the same. Blood markers for insulin and glucose tolerance and hormonal changes were favorable in weight loss cycles in the yo-yo group. Despite spending half of their life overweight, the yo-yo group still benefited from the improved metabolic changes that occurred during dieting. Chronic dieting did not have any adverse effects on lifespan.

Obviously the ability to expand these findings to other animals and humans is limited. Such studies are limited in longer-lived animals, and human studies seldom span more than 25 to 30 years.

But other related research may indicate that these findings are relevant to other species.

Dieting Shows Immediate Benefits

Massive amounts of research in many animal species and humans document the immediate beneficial effects of weight loss. Blood markers for insulin and glucose tolerance, and favorable metabolic and hormonal changes immediately improve. Fat inflammatory markers immediately decrease. There is little doubt that these positive changes would have beneficial health effects and possibly improve lifespan outcomes. Also, studies in dogs and cats substantiate that the chronic overweight or obese state does indeed shorten lifespans by almost two years. Human studies also suggest that obesity significantly impacts lifespan.

So we know that no matter how often or how much we work to control weight it has a positive health effect. We know that if we do nothing, a shortened lifespan is a probable certainty. What we don't know is how much time being spent overweight or obese is enough to affect lifespan. Future research may or may not answer this question for us or our pets.

If we are like the mice, then 50% of our lives spent overweight or obese is not enough to shorten life. So is it 60–75% or 76–99%? Or are we and our pets *unlike* mice and less than 50% of our lives spent overweight or obese is enough to affect our lifespans? We may never know.

What we do know is that doing nothing is not an option. No matter whether our efforts lead to permanent success, we can only help ourselves and our pets by the continued efforts. Any and all attempts to lose weight and eat healthy in the New Year will help. Good luck.

FIVE

It Is Not Necessary to Lose Weight to Be Healthy

Linda Bacon

> Linda Bacon is a nutrition professor in the Biology Department at City College of San Francisco. She holds a doctorate in physiology, specializing in weight regulation, from the University of California–Davis and is the author of *Health at Every Size: The Surprising Truth About Your Weight.* In the following viewpoint Bacon argues that current research shows obesity in itself does not cause early death or serious health problems. She also cites research that found that people who accept their bodies are more likely to eat more-healthful foods and to exercise, compared with those who are trying to lose weight. Other research shows that recent initiatives to promote weight-loss in children and adults have failed and have led to increased stigmatization of overweight people and weight-based discrimination—which lead to eating disorders and other mental health issues. Bacon suggests accepting and caring for one's body as the route to health.

*A*mericans are fatter than they used to be. . . . *Everyone knows the weight is causing sickness and early death. Government and industry say the pounds are costing us. . . . This generation will have* *shorter lives than their parents. . . . Studies show long-term weight loss elusive. . . . Doctors say to keep trying anyway. . . .*

Does it ever seem like you're hearing the same things about weight over and over? Witnessing the depressing cycle of failed public initiatives and fruitless personal efforts to trim our waistlines, who wouldn't wish for a more hopeful angle or some alternative facts on the old story?

Fortunately, an alternative viewpoint is out there, and those facts are available, even if they can be hard to hear over the societal clamor of food fear and body bias. Getting to this information requires tuning out the loud "everyone knows" claims about obesity, shape and diet. It means questioning health "experts" who themselves have failed to question. It requires adopting a new, more skeptical mantra, like the one we use in the movement known as Health at Every Size® (HAES). "Show me the data," we demand, and you should, too.

Focus on Health Rather than on Weight

HAES advocates include scientists, doctors, therapists, dietitians, fitness professionals, and writers, among others. If more doctors, journalists and public officials were to seek their wisdom, they would do less harm, save tax dollars, and help people live longer, healthier and better.

I see information every day that shows that our obsession over body fat is a costly, crippling threat to health and well-being. I routinely tally the costs—medical, financial and psychological—of the un-winnable War on Obesity and the commercial juggernaut it supports (Low-cal snacks! Diet pills! Weight-loss centers where customers always come back!). And I conduct research and write peer-reviewed articles supporting the HAES paradigm with facts, replacing knee-jerk *everyone knows* statements with what is truly known about the meaning of body weight.

The evidence demonstrates that fat isn't the bogeyman it's made out to be, and that a focus on health habits, rather than weight, accomplishes the very goals collective thinness is supposed to achieve (if it were possible in the first place). Compared

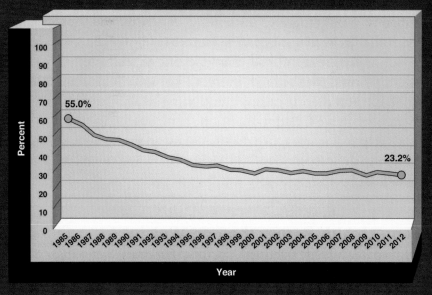

Percentage of Americans Who Find Being Overweight Unattractive, 1985–2012

In polls conducted by the NPD Group since 1985, the percentage of Americans who agree with the statement "People who are not overweight look a lot more attractive" has declined dramatically.

55.0%

23.2%

Percent

1985 1986 1987 1988 1989 1990 1991 1992 1993 1994 1995 1996 1997 1998 1999 2000 2001 2002 2003 2004 2005 2006 2007 2008 2009 2010 2011 2012

Year

Taken from: "The NPD Group Reports Dieting Is at an All Time Low Dieting Season Has Begun, but It's Not What It Used to Be!" NPD.com, January 7, 2013. www.npd.com/wps/portal/npd/us/news/press-releases/the-npd-group -reports-dieting-is-at-an-all-time-low-dieting-season-has-begun-but-its-not-what-it-used-to-be/.

to control groups of people on weight loss programs, people who accept themselves and their bodies as they are tend to exercise more and eat better. They do better medically, on blood pressure, cholesterol, insulin sensitivity and similar measures, and feel happier in the long run. They adopt longer-lasting exercise habits. And guess which group weighs less, two years out? Neither! In the HAES study I conducted, both groups ended up with weights where they started, albeit with the dieters having endured another wearying and health-damaging deprivation-loss-regain cycle.

Evidence-Based Policies

In other words, as long as we're focused on changing our bodies—which the data shows isn't going to happen for most people, anyway—we are missing the real benefits that come from *caring for* our bodies.

Every week or month, another example emerges of knee-jerk assumptions about what *everyone knows*, rather than what we actually do know, shaping decisions in medicine and government. Despite all the talk about "evidence-based" policy, for instance, Medicare is now covering doctor-prescribed weight-loss efforts while the evidence clearly shows that they don't improve health or result in sustained weight loss. The First Lady [Michelle Obama] is devoting herself to eradicating childhood obesity, when the latest meta-analysis of 55 interventions showed an approximate mean weight loss of . . . one pound. These "health" initiatives have not just failed, they've backfired, contributing to the rise in weight-based discrimination and bullying, among many other damaging side effects.

What is known (even if everyone can't accept it yet) is that:

- Stable fat is blown out of proportion as a health risk (even dreaded "tummy fat"), but yo-yoing weights common to dieters *do* harm health.
- The "ironclad" notion that obesity leads to early death is wrong: Mortality data show "overweight" people, on average, live longest, and moderately "obese" people have similar longevity to those at weights deemed "normal" and advisable.
- Life spans have lengthened almost in lockstep with waistlines over the last few decades, which should make you wonder about the supposed deadliness of fat.

Stigmatizing Obesity

When you consider our cultural preoccupation with food and weight, the data on eating disorders and mental health (among thin people, too), and the social justice concerns that arise from waging a war against body types, fat stigma ranks as far more dangerous than rolls and rolls of fat. And when you see who earns what from the billions spent annually on weight-loss products, procedures, and pharmaceuticals, it becomes clear that commercial interests have tainted obesity beliefs, policy and research. (As a small example, take those controversial fat kid ads in Georgia;

Recent research has found that people who accept their bodies as they are are more likely to eat more-healthful foods and to exercise more than are those who are trying to lose weight to attain a certain body image.

the for-profit health care company behind them also sells costly, unproven lap-band surgery to teenagers.)

Let me interject here that I know this post will bring out the usual crew of haters, bashers, the data-resistant, and the sanctimonious "I-lost-weight-and-you-can-too" testimonials in the comments section. For those tempted to participate, I say, "YOU are the obesity problem. But help is available." Any argument you can come up with, someone in the HAES or Fat Acceptance communities has already responded. Read the research review, or my discussion of fat vs. fat stigma for starters, and check out many more resources available on my website [www.lindabacon .org/] or read my book, *Health at Every Size: The Surprising Truth about Your Weight*. That world view is on the wane.

Based on real evidence, all these experts reject a fat focus in favor of more hopeful, more effective, and cheaper paths to good health. No matter what everyone knows, or says they do, HAES experts follow the evidence that it's how you live, not how you look, that makes the difference for health and well-being.

SIX

The Government Has an Important Role to Play in Combating Obesity

Pamela Peeke, as told to Katy Waldman

Journalist Katy Waldman is a reporter for *Slate*, an award-winning online daily magazine. In the following selection Waldman interviews Pamela Peeke, a physician, chief life-style expert at the health-information website WebMD, and author of *Body for Life for Women* and *Fit to Live*. Peeke argues that the government has a strong role to play in promoting health and reducing obesity. While she doesn't believe direct regulation (e.g., restricting unhealthful food) is effective or appropriate, she says the government could be doing much more to promote research and communicate to the public what is being discovered about how to effectively deal with obesity. Peeke would like to see the public constantly exposed—via TV, radio, and the Internet—to useful information about factors that influence health and obesity, such as exercise, food, stress, and the environment. Another important role the government should play, Peeke asserts, is in creating infrastructure that promotes health; such as parks, sidewalks, and organic gardens.

Waldman: Let's start with the burning question. Is obesity a choice?

Peeke: Obesity is not a choice. It's a complex situation, an interplay of countless factors. It can involve a potential in people's lives—they have a potential for being obese, perhaps through genetic lines, but by controlling other variables, they can dampen that significantly. This is a matter of awareness, enlightenment, and being equipped with the appropriate tips, tools, and techniques. You're not just some passive person whom obesity whacks in the head. It may not be your fault that you have whatever genetic or environmental cards you have, but it is within your domain to make some choices that will help control your weight.

So obesity is not a choice, but it's possible to make choices that prevent you from being obese?

Yes, and it's possible to lose weight despite being genetically predisposed to obesity. I have legions of patients who have done this. It takes *mental* and *physical* fitness: I link the two all the time. I have to. I'm tired of people treating the body like a dog you take for a run.

What is mental fitness? Is it willpower?

It's more than that. Current research shows that a strengthened prefrontal cortex from physical activity allows you to rein in impulsivity. You don't need more than 30–45 minutes of walking a day to get the effects. Also, people who do regular physical activity can dampen the effect of the FTO gene, which is a very powerful gene associated with obesity, by 40 percent.

Let's say you're born with the worst genes on the planet and you feel *doomed*, like you just want to eat a lot. If you exercise on a regular basis (as well as meditate, by the way), you'll make the right choices more often. You'll be more mindful and less impulsive.

The Role of Government in Combating Obesity

Where does the government come in?

I am not advocating for a nanny state. I don't want someone taking my mother's chocolate-chip cookie out of my hand.

Woman's health expert Pamela Peeke (pictured) argues that the government has a strong role to play in promoting health and reducing obesity.

Oh my God, it's a food felony! I mean, that's ridiculous. I'll just score it somewhere else. But there's a lot the government can do. Number one is promoting research. Last time I looked, the National Institutes of Health had a congressional budget. We need to use that budget to understand the underpinnings, the hot new research that's coming out. Another thing we need is education at 900 different levels—from the Department of Health and Human Services to the Centers for Disease Control [and Prevention] to the U.S. Food and Drug Administration [FDA]. We need it to be free, easily accessed, easily digested. I'd love to see more education platforms on television, radio, and the Internet. People should constantly be hearing appropriate information about food, physical activity, environment, stress, and everything else that can contribute to the obesity epidemic.

But there's so much information already out there. Do you think it's made a difference?

People are not making the connections. You're motivated to change when you see a greater reward in doing something else. That's why the way in which the information is communicated is absolutely critical. If you give the best information in a dry format, I don't care how right it is—it's very hard to digest and to relate to your own life. Talking about health is lethally boring. If you and I start talking shoes, we could talk for hours. It stirs up this pleasure in our minds. But now, when I flip the conversation over to obesity, there's dead silence, right? As a communicator, my job is to turn the boring factoids into what I love to call simple, sexy, sticky sound bites. You make it so interesting and fun that someone says, "Oh my god. I never knew that."

Here's another thing the government can do better: infrastructure. As a citizen, I can't create a park or make sidewalks happen when they're not there. We should have tons and tons of voluntary campaigns, such as the Presidential Active Lifestyle Award and Let's Move, which get people inspired without ramming it up their nose. We've got dead land just sitting around in Detroit, in all kinds of places. Why couldn't the government take some of that land and convert it into organic gardens? Science shows that when children grow their own, they eat their own, meaning that if they grew that zucchini, they're going to eat it with pride.

The War on Obesity

Why frame any of this as a war on obesity? Why not just encourage people to move more and eat better?

You're asking, I think, whether "healthy" and "overweight" are mutually exclusive. It's really about where you start. Twenty-five years ago, someone with 20 pounds to drop was in dire straits. Today, physicians get people with over 100 pounds to drop. Let's say I'm working with an average-heighted woman of about 220 pounds. There's not a single person who thinks a 5-foot-4 woman should be north of 200; that's just ridiculous. So we really concentrate on getting out of that red zone. Now I've got her down to 160 pounds. She's physically fit, just ran a 10K [10 kilometer race], but you know, her little body, it's rough. She's not going any lower, and the BMI [body mass index] says she's overweight. But she's actually in better shape than someone who is 130 pounds and 5-foot-4 and never exercises and eats trash.

Of course, if you're currently average-weighted—the three of you left in the United States—I'm all about obesity *prevention*. I'll say, "Come on now. Grow up. Eat your whole foods, be physically active, learn better stress management, meditate, whatever."

The Unfair Stigma Against Obese People

Do you agree with . . . Paul Campos that the obese are unfairly stigmatized?

Oh, yes. When I say things like "Grow up," I'm being facetious. Obese people are living in hell. They can't find decent clothes. Most people stereotype them on multiple levels. They've got self-denigration, poor body image, all the rest of it. What you want to do is show them tremendous compassion. At the same time, educate them. Give them credible tools to be able to help themselves. We do this with smoking all the time, providing drugs, patches, cessation programs, and apps. But unlike with smoking, [obese people] need a team behind them that understands the risks and in a very compassionate way offers appropriate, palatable, doable programs.

An obese white woman makes $1,855 less, on average, than a white woman in the normal BMI range. How can the government combat fat discrimination?

Percentage of Americans Favoring a Significant Government Role in Combating Childhood Obesity, 2011

In a poll conducted by the Pew Research Center in 2011, a majority of respondents believed the government should have a significant role in reducing childhood obesity.

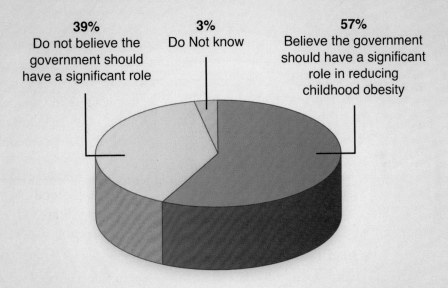

39%
Do not believe the government should have a significant role

3%
Do Not know

57%
Believe the government should have a significant role in reducing childhood obesity

Taken from: "Most See Role for Government in Reducing Childhood Obesity." Pew Research Center for the People and the Press, March 8, 2011. www.people-press.org/2011/03/08/most-see-role-for-government-in-reducing -childhood-obesity/.

They can combat it to the degree that if someone in your office were interviewing people and overtly refused to hire someone on account of her weight, that's illegal. Of course that happens very rarely. Far more often, you have five candidates, two of whom are obese, and neither of the obese people get the job. The bias is streaming quietly in the background.

One place to start is popular culture. Look at that show on television now, *Mike and Molly*. Can you imagine it airing 30 years ago? Never! And suddenly there they are, and they're funny and cute and also struggling with their weight, and they both know it. They say it out loud. And they're bringing obesity out of the closet. You can't regulate the way people are thinking, but you can change the culture, change the language.

Communication Versus Regulation

What do you think about how pop culture currently defines the ideal body?

Oh, for women? Far too thin.

If the government can regulate junk food advertisements on the grounds that they promote harmful habits, should it be able to regulate ads that celebrate dangerously skinny women?

What really needs to happen is that leaders in the industry, like [US fashion designer] Donna Karan, need to stand up and speak out. They need to start hiring healthy-looking models and paying them well. . . .

Are there any food products sold today with no redeeming value whatsoever?

It's interesting that you say "redeeming value," because people like to have balance and freedom of choice. If they want to have a fried Twinkie at some county fair, I'm going to cringe, because I think Twinkies are science fair projects. I don't know what they are. But they're someone else's treat.

What really horrifies me is when they take a regular hamburger and turn it into this 5,000 calorie stack of everything. It's a heart attack in a gigantic pile. There is nothing wrong with a decent burger, but piling it up for 20 stories is completely absurd. Your body is not going to like what you just did to it. I don't care how young you are.

Should the 20-story burger be banned or regulated?

No. That tack is only appropriate in the context of dietary supplements, where you see absolute harm to life and body. Aside from the FDA protecting me from pharmaceutical scams, I am against regulation. I support the government continuing to take nonregulatory roles, but *doing them better*. For instance, agencies are communicating now, but it's so boring I could shoot myself. Where is the social media? Where is the Facebook page explaining USDA [US Department of Agriculture] labels?

SEVEN

Synthetic Chemicals That Disrupt Metabolism May Be Contributing to the Obesity Epidemic

Laura Fraser

Laura Fraser is a journalist based in San Francisco, California, and the author of *Losing It: America's Obsession with Weight and the Industry That Feeds on It*. In the following viewpoint Fraser suggests that a class of chemicals known as endocrine disruptors may play a role in increased levels of obesity in the United States. These synthetic chemicals, which are now widely distributed in the human environment, closely resemble natural hormones and therefore may interfere with normal metabolism and development. The author reports that when pregnant mice were fed some of these chemicals, their offspring had 10 percent more fat cells and weighed 10 percent more than a typical mouse. Other research has shown that many animals that live close to humans become fatter than animals that do not—even in the case of laboratory animals whose exercise and food are closely monitored and controlled.

We all know that Americans—leading the way for the rest of the developed world—are getting fatter. We hear about the "obesity epidemic" on the TV news, with footage of people depicted from the waist down shuffling around in XXL sweatpants and carrying supersized sodas. The majority of us are overweight, complaining about how our jeans are getting tighter and wondering why; despite all our efforts to diet and go to the gym, the number on the scale keeps edging higher.

For years, the explanation for weight gain was straightforward: it was all about energy balance, or calories-in versus calories-out. This Gluttony and Sloth theory held that obesity simply came from overeating and underexercising, and the only debate was about dieting—whether it was better to join the low-fat or the low-carb camp. Some scientists explored genetic differences associated with fat, but others said genes couldn't possibly explain the rate at which Americans were gaining weight: "We just aren't evolving that fast," one obesity expert noted.

Environmental Factors Affecting Obesity

Environmental scientists have long suggested that there were likely external factors at work, but until recently, the traditional obesity-research community rejected such claims. Now it seems that the tide is turning: This month's [June 2011] issue of *Obesity Reviews* features an extensive look at the accumulating body of research linking the environment with obesity.

The idea of our surroundings contributing to weight gain is nothing new, of course. But past discussions about the role of the "environment" focused mostly on the fast-food culture that we live in, where highly processed, highly caloric foods are constantly available, eating times are chaotic, kids run around drinking sugar-saturated sodas all day, no one has time to cook, fruits and vegetables are scarce in low-income urban areas, a venti frappuccino has 760 calories, and muffins are the size of melons. Add to that our changing physical environment—the fact that everyone sits in front of computers every day, instead of working out or working on the farm—and the "calories in" excess of the weight equation seems obvious, and obesity over-determined.

But even allowing for such influences, something wasn't adding up. There are plenty of people out there who eat well and exercise like [rail-thin actress] Gwyneth Paltrow and still feel like their weight is out of control. Then there are those annoying people who eat everything they desire, never work out, and stay thin. There had to be more to it than calories. We know that hormones—the chemical messengers produced by our endocrine system to control things like blood pressure and insulin production—can fatten up animals for slaughter; that some drugs increase your weight; and that a change in hormones at midlife shifts where your fat is distributed. Researchers began to recognize that obesity is much more complicated than calories in and out, and that a lot of other mechanisms involving the hormonal regulatory system are involved in our bodies' delicate weight balance.

Paula Baillie-Hamilton, an expert on metabolism and environmental toxins at Stirling University in Scotland, was among the first to make the link between the obesity epidemic and the increase in the chemicals in our lives. "Overlooked in the obesity debate," she wrote in 2002 in the *Journal of Alternative and Complementary Medicine*, "is that the earth's environment has changed significantly during the last few decades because of the exponential production and usage of synthetic organic and inorganic chemicals."

"Chemical Calories"

Exposure to those chemicals, said Baillie-Hamilton, can damage the body's natural weight-control mechanisms. She calls toxic chemicals that act as endocrine disruptors—mimicking hormones, and blocking or exaggerating our natural hormonal responses— "chemical calories," and those in question include Bisphenol A, phthalates, PCBs [polychlorinated biphenyls], persistant organic pollutants such as DDE, a breakdown product of the insecticide DDT, and pesticides containing tin compounds called organotins. Many studies have shown that endocrine disruptors have been linked to early puberty, impaired immune function, different types of cancer, birth deformities, and other diseases. Now obesity and metabolism are on that list.

Various pesticides that contain endocrine disruptors are shown in laboratory containers. Many studies have shown that endocrine disruptors have been linked to health problems such as early puberty, impaired immune function, different types of cancer, birth deformities, and obesity.

Environmental researchers call these chemical calories "obesogens." Bruce Blumberg, a University of California at Irvine professor of developmental and cell biology, studies the effects of endocrine disruptors on obesity in mice and sees clear differences between those who are exposed to them and those who aren't. "Pretty much anyone who observes people knows that obesity is way more than eating and exercise," says Blumberg. Instead, metabolism, appetite, and the number and size of fat cells you have come into play, all of which are affected by hormones, and therefore by hormone disruptors. Blumberg has shown that the organic pollutants tributyltin and triphenyltin derail the hormonal mechanisms that control the weight of mice. He's found that when pregnant mice are fed a dose of organotins that is equivalent to normal human exposure to those chemicals, their offspring have 10 percent more fat cells than normal mice, the fat cells grow bigger than normal, and they end up, overall, 10 percent fatter than your average mouse.

Other compelling research that fat is not just about eating and exercise comes from studies that show that animals that live in human environments get fatter just by virtue of being around people. Researchers at the University of Alabama recently found that chimpanzees, macaques [monkeys], mice, rats, dogs, cats, and other species that lived in proximity to humans got fatter than animals that didn't live in an industrialized environment—even when their lab chow and exercise was highly controlled. The authors suggested that endocrine disruptors were one likely culprit in this cross-species obesity epidemic.

For her article in the new *Obesity Reviews*, Jeanett Tang-Peronard, of the Institute of Preventive Medicine in Copenhagen, [Denmark,] looked at some 450 studies on endocrine disruptors and obesity and found that nearly all of them showed a correlation between exposure to those chemicals—particularly *in utero* ["in the womb"; i.e., before birth] and in early childhood, when hormonal mechanisms are vulnerable—and an increase in body size. She says that in early life, chemicals seem to alter the . . . regulation of certain genes, disrupting the programming of hormonal signaling pathways that affect fat storage, fat distribution, and appetite. . . .

Reducing Exposure to Hormone Disruptors

Tang-Peronard says that it is impossible, now, to tease out how much of obesity is caused by chemicals, and how much by energy balance. They're intertwined, anyway, with imbalances in appetite-regulating hormones like leptin and ghrelin causing us to want to eat more of the available food. "Endocrine disruptors may play a significant role in obesity," she says. But the research is in its infancy. She also points out that only a few of the tens of thousands of known environmental chemicals have been tested for their association with obesity. "We are only scratching the surface," she says.

What to do about the problem of endocrine disruptors and obesity? It's hard to say, given that virtually all humans have been exposed. Pediatrician Maida Galvez is involved in the Mt. Sinai [Hospital] "Growing Up Healthy" study of 330 children in East Harlem [New York], monitoring their exposure to endo-

Changes in the Prevalence of Adult Obesity in Nine Countries

Over several decades the percentage of the population that is obese (defined as having a body mass index of thirty or more) has increased steadily in many countries around the world. Some researchers believe the culprit may be chemical pollutants in the environment that interfere with normal metabolism.

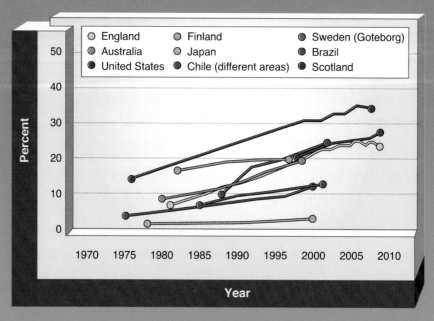

Taken from: Sarah McLusky, Rosina Malagrida, and Lorena Valverde. "The Genetics of Obesity: A Lab Activity." Science in School, February 20, 2013. www.scienceinschool.org/2013/issue26/obesity.

crine disruptors and their body weight. "Even if these chemicals play a small role in obesity, it's a preventable exposure," she says, explaining that if certain substances can be determined to have deleterious effects, we can avoid them at critical stages of development and ultimately replace them with safer alternatives.

For now, Galvez recommends that parents steer clear of Bisphenol-A—present in many plastic water and baby bottles, and in microwavable and dishwasher-safe food containers. (If you find a printed "7" on the bottom, get rid of it.) She also suggests avoiding shampoos, cosmetics, and soaps containing phthalates—up to 70 percent of "top-selling products," according to a 2002 report by the Environmental Working Group. (Look for fragrance-free products, which are less likely to contain phthalates, or for anything from the Illumina Organics range or The Body Shop.) And, she says, eat fresh fruits and vegetables, instead of foods that are processed and/or packaged in plastic.

That's one point on which traditional obesity researchers and environmental scientists agree: Eat plenty of fresh, organic vegetables. And while you're at it, get out into the fresh air and get some exercise.

EIGHT

Why the Campaign to Stop America's Obesity Crisis Keeps Failing

Gary Taubes

Gary Taubes is a Robert Wood Johnson Foundation independent investigator in Health Policy Research at the University of California and the author of *Good Calories, Bad Calories: Challenging the Conventional Wisdom on Diet, Weight Control and Disease*. In the following selection Taubes refutes the popular wisdom that obesity is solely caused by people consuming more calories than they burn through exercise. The real cause of obesity, he claims, is an excess of refined grains and sugars in the US diet. The author says research has shown that such foods cause an excess production of insulin and a corresponding accumulation of fat. According to Taubes, this explains a high rate of childhood obesity in the United States during the Great Depression of the 1930s, when food was scarce but the diet consisted mostly of sugars, refined flour, and starches.

Most of my favorite factoids about obesity are historical ones, and they don't make it into the new, four-part HBO documentary on the subject, *The Weight of the Nation*. Absent, for instance, is the fact that the very first childhood-obesity clinic in the United States was founded in the late 1930s at Columbia University by a young German physician, Hilde Bruch. As Bruch later told it, her inspiration was simple: she arrived in New York in 1934 and was "startled" by the number of fat kids she saw—"really fat ones, not only in clinics, but on the streets and subways, and in schools."

What makes Bruch's story relevant to the obesity problem today is that this was New York in the worst year of the Great Depression, an era of bread lines and soup kitchens, when 6 in 10 Americans were living in poverty. The conventional wisdom these days—promoted by government, obesity researchers, physicians, and probably your personal trainer as well—is that we get fat because we have too much to eat and not enough reasons to be physically active. But then why were the PC- and Big Mac–deprived Depression-era kids fat? How can we blame the obesity epidemic on gluttony and sloth if we easily find epidemics of obesity throughout the past century in populations that barely had food to survive and had to work hard to earn it?

These seem like obvious questions to ask, but you won't get the answers from the anti-obesity establishment, which this month has come together to unfold a major anti-fat effort, including *The Weight of the Nation*, which begins airing May 14 and "a nationwide community-based outreach campaign." The project was created by a coalition among HBO and three key public-health institutions: the nonprofit Institute of Medicine, and two federal agencies, the Centers for Disease Control and Prevention and the National Institutes of Health. Indeed, it is unprecedented to have the IOM, CDC, and NIH all supporting a single television documentary, says producer John Hoffmann. The idea is to "sound the alarm" and motivate the nation to act.

At its heart is a simple "energy balance" idea: we get fat because we consume too many calories and expend too few. If we could just control our impulses—or at least control our environment, thereby removing temptation—and push ourselves to exercise, we'd be fine. This logic is everywhere you look in the official guidelines, commentary, and advice. "The same amount of energy IN and energy OUT over time = weight stays the same," the

NIH website counsels Americans, while the CDC site tells us, "Overweight and obesity result from an energy imbalance."

The problem is, the solutions this multi-level campaign promotes are the same ones that have been used to fight obesity for a century—and they just haven't worked. "We are struggling to figure this out," NIH Director Francis Collins conceded to *Newsweek* last week. When I interviewed CDC obesity expert William Dietz back in 2001, he told me that his primary accomplishment had been getting childhood obesity "on the map." "It's now widely recognized as a major health problem in the United States," he said then—and that was 10 years and a few million obese children ago.

There is an alternative theory, one that has also been around for decades but that the establishment has largely ignored. This theory implicates specific foods—refined sugars and grains—because of their effect on the hormone insulin, which regulates fat accumulation. If this hormonal-defect hypothesis is true, not all calories are created equal, as the conventional wisdom holds. And if it is true, the problem is not only controlling our impulses, but also changing the entire American food economy and rewriting our beliefs about what constitutes a healthy diet.

Oddly, this nutrient-hormone-fat interaction is not particularly controversial. You can find it in medical textbooks as the explanation for why our fat cells get fat. But the anti-obesity establishment doesn't take the next step: that fat fat cells lead to fat humans. In their eyes, yes, insulin regulates how much fat gets trapped in your fat cells, and the kinds of carbohydrates we eat today pretty much drive up your insulin levels. But, they conclude, while individual cells get fat that way, the reason an entire human gets fat has nothing to do with it. We're just eating too much.

I've been arguing otherwise. And one reason I like this hormonal hypothesis of obesity is that it explains the fat kids in Depression-era New York. As the extreme situation of exceedingly poor populations shows, the problem could not have been that they ate too much, because they didn't have enough food available. The problem then—as now, across America—was the

Sugar, Diabetes, and Obesity, 1980 and 2010

Between 1980 and 2010 the amount of sugar in the US diet increased significantly, as had the prevalence of obesity and diabetes.

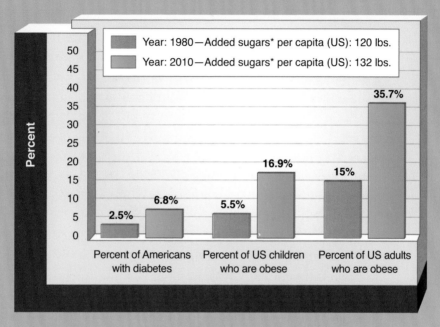

Legend:
- Year: 1980—Added sugars* per capita (US): 120 lbs.
- Year: 2010—Added sugars* per capita (US): 132 lbs.

Percent of Americans with diabetes: 2.5%, 6.8%
Percent of US children who are obese: 5.5%, 16.9%
Percent of US adults who are obese: 15%, 35.7%

*Includes sugars, corn sweeteners, honey, and syrups.

Taken from: Gary Taubes and Cristin Kearns Couzens. "Big Sugar's Sweet Little Lies." *Mother Jones*, November/December 2012. www.motherjones.com/environment/2012/10/sugar-industry-lies-campaign.

prevalence of sugars, refined flour, and starches in their diets. These are the cheapest calories, and they can be plenty tasty without a lot of preparation and preservation. And the biology suggests that they are literally fattening—they make us fat, while other foods (fats, proteins, and green leafy vegetables) don't.

If this hypothesis is right, then the reason the anti-obesity efforts championed by the IOM, the CDC, and the NIH haven't worked and won't work is not because we're not listening, and not because we just can't say no, but because these efforts are not addressing the fundamental cause of the problem. Like trying to prevent lung cancer by getting smokers to eat less and run more, it won't work because the intervention is wrong.

The authority figures in obesity and nutrition are so fixed on the simplistic calorie-balance idea that they're willing to ignore virtually any science to hold on to it.

The first and most obvious mistake they make is embracing the notion that the only way foods can influence how fat we get is through the amount of energy—calories—they contain. The iconic example here is sugar, or rather sugars, since we're talking about both sucrose (the white, granulated stuff we sprinkle on cereal) and high-fructose corn syrup. "What's the single best thing I can do for me and my family?" asks one obese mother in *The Weight of the Nation*. The answer she's given is "stop drinking sugar-sweetened beverages." But the official wisdom—that all we need know is that a calorie is a calorie is a calorie—doesn't explain why that might be so.

Left unsaid is the fact that sucrose and high-fructose corn syrup have a unique chemical composition, a near 50-50 combination of two different carbohydrates: glucose and fructose. And while glucose is metabolized by virtually every cell in the body, the fructose (also found in fruit, but in much lower concentrations) is metabolized mostly by liver cells. From there, the chain of metabolic events has been worked out by biochemists over 50 years: some of the fructose is converted into fat, the fat accumulates in the liver cells, which become resistant to the action of insulin, and so more insulin is secreted to compensate. The end results are elevated levels of insulin, which is the hallmark of type 2 diabetes, and the steady accumulation of fat in our fat tissue—a few tens of calories worth per day, leading to pounds per year, and obesity over the course of a few decades.

Last fall, researchers at the University of California, Davis, published three studies—two of humans, one of rhesus monkeys—confirming the deleterious effect of these sugars on metabolism and insulin levels. The message of all three studies was that sugars are unhealthy—not because people or monkeys consumed too much of them, but because, well, they do things to our bodies that the other nutrients we eat simply don't do.

The second fallacy is the belief that physical activity plays a meaningful role in keeping off the pounds—an idea that the authorities just can't seem to let go of, despite all evidence to the contrary. "We don't walk, we don't bike," says University of North Carolina economist Barry Popkin in *The Weight of the Nation*. If we do exercise regularly, the logic goes, then we'll at least maintain a healthy weight (along with other health benefits), which is why the official government recommendations from the USDA are that we should all do 150 minutes each week of "moderate intensity" aerobic exercise. And if that's not enough to maintain a healthy weight or lose the excess, then, well, we should do more.

So why is the world full of obese individuals who do exercise regularly? Arkansas construction workers in *The Weight of the Nation*, for instance, do jobs that require constant lifting and running up ladders with "about 50 to 60 pounds of tools"—and an equal amount of excess fat. They're on-camera making the point about how the combination is exhausting. "By the time the day's over," one tells us, "your feet are killing you; your legs are cramping. You can't last as long as you used to." If physical activity helps us lose weight or even just maintain it, how did these hardworking men get so fat?

There are two obvious reasons why this idea that working out makes you skinny or keeps you skinny is likely to be just wrong. One is that it takes a significant amount of exercise to burn even a modest amount of calories. Run three miles, says Cornell University researcher Brian Wansink in the documentary, and you'll burn up roughly the amount of calories in a single candy bar. And this brings up the second reason: you're likely to be hungrier after strenuous exercise than before and so you're more likely to eat that candy bar's worth of calories after than before. (When the American Heart Association and the American College of Sports Medicine jointly published physical-activity guidelines back in 2007, they described the evidence that exercise can even prevent us from growing fatter as "not particularly compelling," which was a kind way to put it.)

Finally, the anti-obesity establishment embraces the idea that what are really missing from our diet are fresh fruits and vegetables— that these are the *sine qua non* of a healthy diet—and that meat,

Research has shown that eating refined sugar causes an excess production of insulin and a corresponding accumulation of fat.

red meat in particular, is a likely cause of obesity. Since the mid-1970s, health agencies have waged a campaign to reduce our meat consumption, for a host of reasons: it causes colon cancer or heart disease (because of the saturated fat) and now because it supposedly makes us fat as well. The lowly cheeseburger is consistently targeted as a contributor to both obesity and diabetes.

But when David Wallinga of the Institute for Agriculture and Trade Policy tells us in *The Weight of the Nation* that the USDA has established the cause of the obesity epidemic and it's "an increase in our calorie consumption over the last 30, 35 years," he also tells us where those calories come from: a quarter come from added sugars, a quarter from added fats ("most of which are from soy"), and "almost half is from refined grains, mainly corn starches, wheat, and the like." What Wallinga doesn't say is that the same USDA data clearly shows that red-meat consumption peaked in this country in the mid-1970s, before the obesity epidemic started. It's been dropping ever since, consistent with a nation that has been doing exactly what health authorities have been telling it to do.

At the moment, the government efforts to curb obesity and diabetes avoid the all-too-apparent fact, as Hilde Bruch pointed out more than half a century ago, that exhorting obese people to eat less and exercise more doesn't work, and that this shouldn't be an indictment of their character but of the value of the advice. By institutionalizing this advice as public-health policy, we waste enormous amounts of money and effort on programs that might make communities nicer places to live—building parks and making green markets available—but that we have little reason to believe will make anyone thinner. When I asked CDC Director Thomas Frieden about this, he pointed to two recent reports, from Massachusetts and New York, documenting small but real decreases in childhood-obesity levels. He then admitted that they had no idea why this had happened. "I'm doing everything I can do," he said, "to assure that we rigorously monitor the efforts underway so we can try to understand what works and what doesn't."

If the latest research is any indication, sugar may have been the primary problem all along. Back in the 1980s, the FDA gave sugar a free pass based on the idea that the evidence wasn't conclusive. While the government spent hundreds of millions trying to prove that salt and saturated fat are bad for our health, it spent virtually nothing on sugar. Had it targeted sugar then, instead of waiting for an obesity and diabetes epidemic for motivation, our entire food culture and the options that go with it might have changed as they did with low-fat and low-salt foods.

So what should we eat? The latest clinical trials suggest that all of us would benefit from fewer (if any) sugars and fewer refined grains (bread, pasta) and starchy vegetables (potatoes). This was the conventional wisdom through the mid-1960s, and then we turned the grains and starches into heart-healthy diet foods and the USDA enshrined them in the base of its famous Food Guide Pyramid as the staples of our diet. That this shift coincides with the obesity epidemic is probably not a coincidence. As for those of us who are overweight, experimental trials, the gold standard of medical evidence, suggest that diets that are severely restricted in fattening carbohydrates and rich in animal products—meat, eggs, cheese—and green leafy vegetables are arguably the best approach, if not the healthiest diet to eat. Not only does weight go down when people eat like this, but heart disease and diabetes risk factors are reduced. Ethical arguments against meat-eating are always valid; health arguments against it can no longer be defended.

If *The Weight of the Nation* accomplishes anything, it's communicating the desperation of obese Americans trying to understand their condition and, even more, of lean (or relatively lean) parents trying to cope with the obesity of their offspring. Lack of will isn't their problem. It's the absence of advice that might actually work. If our authorities on this subject could accept that maybe their fundamental understanding of the problem needs to be rethought, we and they might begin to make progress. Clearly the conventional wisdom has failed so far. We can hold onto it only so long.

NINE

The "Obesity Epidemic" Is Not a Threat to Public Health

Paul Campos

Paul Campos is a professor of law at the University of Colorado at Boulder and the author of *The Obesity Myth*. In the following viewpoint Campos argues that concerns about an "obesity epidemic" in the United States are misplaced. According to Campos, research from the Centers for Disease Control and Prevention's National Health and Nutrition Examination Survey shows a *lower* rate of mortality among people classified overweight or obese compared with those considered to have a normal weight. Campos also refutes an analysis reported by ABC News in August 2008 that claimed that by the middle of the twenty-first century everyone in the United States will be overweight or obese. According to Campos, this is based on an unreliable statistical technique; the thinnest quartile (quarter) of the population has gained no weight in the last thirty years.

Even by the remarkably mendacious [lying] standards of the "obesity" racket some of the claims in this [ABC News] story ["Study Predicts Obesity Apocalypse by 2030"] are beyond belief.

The most laughable is the idea that by 2048 everybody in the US will be "overweight" or "obese." This result was derived via statistical extrapolation, the crack cocaine of social science analysis

A doctor checks a patient's body mass index (BMI), the ratio of a person's weight to height used to gauge whether a person is overweight or obese.

(by similar methods one could prove that within a few generations Olympic sprinters will be running at speeds that will hurl them into low Earth orbit and everyone in America will have a plasma TV seventeen miles wide).

In fact there has been no weight gain at all over the past 30 years in the thinnest quartile [one quarter of a statistical group] of the population—whatever (poorly understood) factors have caused Americans to weigh more on average now than they did in the 1970s have had very different impacts across the weight spectrum:

thin people have gained no weight, people in the middle weigh 10–15 pounds [more] than they did 30 years ago, while the fattest people have gained a lot of weight, which is exactly what one would expect. Furthermore, as even this story manages to note, there's quite a bit of evidence that the trend toward weight gain in the populace in the 1980s and 1990s seems to have plateaued.

The National Health and Nutrition Examination Survey

But this is a side point. The most significant and symptomatic aspect of this story is its completely uncritical attitude toward the current definitions of "overweight" and "obesity." Those definitons are BMIs [body mass indexes] of 25–29.9 and 30+ respectively. (You can look up your own BMI [at www.nhlbi.nih.gov/guidelines /obesity/BMI/bmicalc.htm], and I encourage you to do so).

I really can't emphasize enough how utterly without scientific foundation these definitions are. This can be shown in a hundred ways, but here's one particularly striking illustration.

The best epidemiological data on the U.S. population is the CDC's [Centers for Disease Control and Prevention's] National Health and Nutrition Examination Survey (NHANES). This is universally recognized as the gold standard for such surveys, in particular because it's a nationally representative sample that directly measures its participants. NHANES has been ongoing since the 1960s; the most recent data that allows for significant followup is from NHANES III, which was assembled in 1988–1994.

Now if we're facing an "apocalypse" because of "overweight" and "obesity," we should see evidence of this in, at the very minimum, increased relative risk of mortality among people in these categories. Here's the relevant data from NHANES III on mortality risk. The following statistics use the mortality risk found among supposedly "normal weight" (*sic*) people (BMI 18.5–24.9) as the referent group. In other words, the mortality risk for this group sets the baseline for comparison to other groups in terms of their mortality risk. A group that has a higher mortality risk than the referent group will have excess deaths over the baseline risk.

A group that has a lower mortality risk will have fewer deaths than would be seen in the group if it had the same mortality risk as the referent group of "normal weight" people.

Most recent excess deaths estimates from NHANES III:

Underweight: 38,456
Normal weight: 0
Overweight: -99,980
Obesity Grade I: -13,865
Obesity Grade II and III: 57,515

Underweight [means] less than 18.5 BMI, normal weight 18.5–24.9, overweight 25–29.9, Obesity Grade I 30–34.9, Obesity Grade II and III 35+. What these numbers mean: In the US population at present, we are seeing about 100,000 fewer deaths per year among "overweight" people than we would if "overweight" people had the same mortality risk as "normal weight" people. Note that *the majority* of people in the US who according to the government's current classifications weigh too much are in this group. The "overweight" category is to the obesity panic what marijuana use is to the drug war: stories about an "epidemic" of fatness depend crucially on classifying the 35% of the population that's "overweight" as being at some sort of increased health risk. This is simply false, and is known to be false by the researchers who are quoted in stories like the one linked above.

Obesity Is Associated with a Lower Risk of Death

But the situation is much more egregious than even this suggests. Note that the NHANES III data reveals that most people who are classified as obese have a lower mortality risk than so-called normal weight people. About two-thirds of "obese" Americans have a BMI of between 30–34.9, and currently we're seeing about 14,000 fewer deaths per year in this group than would be expected if the group's mortality risk was the same as that of "normal weight" individuals.

BMI Body Comparison

BMI (body mass index) is a standard way to measure obesity by calculating a height-to-weight ratio. However, some criticize it as an overly crude and misleading way of estimating obesity. The image depicts two men with a BMI of 33.9, which would be considered obese.

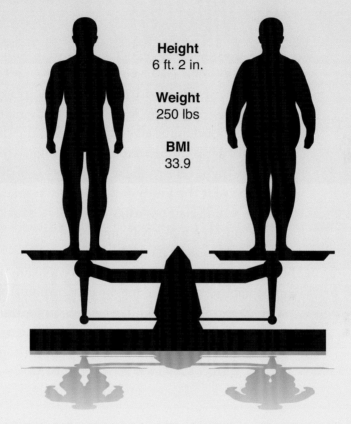

Height
6 ft. 2 in.

Weight
250 lbs

BMI
33.9

Taken from: Stephanie Wilson. "Body Mass Index: Is BMI an Accurate Measure of Obesity?" How Stuff Works. http://health.howstuffworks.com/wellness/diet-fitness/weight-loss/bmi3.htm.

Only when one gets to roughly the fattest 10% of the population does the NHANES III data begin to find a relative mortality risk higher than that found among the supposedly "normal weight." And even here, the relative mortality risk results in about three times fewer deaths per capita than observed among the "underweight" (there are approximately four times as many people with BMIs 35+ than there are people with BMIs below 18.5).

In short, it's difficult to convey the utter intellectual bankruptcy of the standard discourse surrounding weight and health in this culture.

Update addressing a couple of common themes in these sorts of discussions:

(1) I don't think that the higher mortality rate among "normal" (*sic*) or "optimal" (*sic*) weight people provides any real evidence that someone with a BMI in that range should try to gain weight. The bogus idea here is that a narrow range of weight is optimal for all people. In fact the differences in mortality across an extremely broad range (roughly BMIs from the high teens to the mid-30s) are statistically trivial, and represent the kinds of differences in relative risk that nobody would ever pay attention to if not for cultural considerations that make body mass a subject of great symbolic (though not medical) importance.

(2) It really is astonishing how ready people are to accept the most dubious evidence for the proposition that everybody should try to be thin, while engaging in sophisticated arguments about why evidence to the contrary can be explained away. That this blatantly inconsistent attitude is characterized as the essence of science is also rather remarkable.

TEN

The Obesity Epidemic Is a Serious Threat to Public Health

David Katz

David Katz is the founding director of Yale University's Prevention Research Center and coauthor of *Dr. David Katz's Flavor-Full Diet: Use Your Tastebuds to Lose Pounds and Inches with this Scientifically Proven Plan.* In the following selection Katz disputes a study reporting that mild to moderate obesity is associated with a lower mortality rate, which has been taken by some to indicate that obesity is not a serious health concern. Katz says a single study does not disprove the large body of scientific evidence associating obesity with ill health and notes that this study is flawed in several ways—e.g., in failing to take into account that many people are thin not because they are healthy but because of adverse health conditions such as drug addiction or eating disorders. Furthermore, while medical treatments may be able to decrease *mortality*, those who are obese suffer from increased *morbidity*, or disease conditions.

According to a widely circulated op-ed in yesterday's [January 4, 2013,] *New York Times* by Paul Campos, a law professor at the University of Colorado with whom I don't believe I have ever managed to agree on anything, our "fear" of fat—namely, epidemic obesity—is, in a word, absurd. Prof. Campos is the author of a book entitled *The Obesity Myth*, and has established something of a cottage industry for some time contending that the fuss we make about epidemic obesity is all some government-manufactured conspiracy theory, or a confabulation serving the interests of the weight-loss-pharmaceutical complex.

In this instance, the op-ed was reacting to a meta-analysis, published this week in *JAMA* [*Journal of the American Medical Association*], and itself the subject of extensive media attention, indicating that mortality rates go up as obesity gets severe, but that mild obesity and overweight are actually associated with lower overall mortality than so-called "healthy" weight. This study—debunked for important deficiencies by many leading scientists around the country, and with important limitations acknowledged by its own authors—was treated by Prof. Campos as if a third tablet on the summit of Mount Sinai [i.e., in addition to the two tablets containing the Ten Commandments given by God to Moses].

A Deeply Flawed Obesity Study

We'll get into the details of the meta-analysis shortly, but first I'd like to say: Treating science like a ping-pong ball is what's absurd, and what scares the hell out of me. Treating any one study as if its findings annihilate the gradual, hard-earned accumulation of evidence over decades is absurd, and scares the hell out of me. Iconoclasts who get lots of attention just by refuting the conventional wisdom, and who are occasionally and importantly right, but far more often wrong—are often rather absurd, and scare the hell out of me.

And so does the obesity epidemic.

As for the meta-analysis, a study designed to pool the results of other studies, it is in some ways complex and in some ways quite sophisticated. But in many important ways, it is very crude.

A meta-analysis is never any better than the studies it is aggregating. In this case, those studies merely looked at the population-level association between the body mass index [BMI], itself a rather crude measure of body fat—which is what really matters—and death rate.

Trends in the Prevalence of Obesity Among US Children and Adolescents, by Age and Survey Year

Surveys conducted in the United States between 1971 and 2010 show a significant increase in the percentage of children and youth classified as obese.

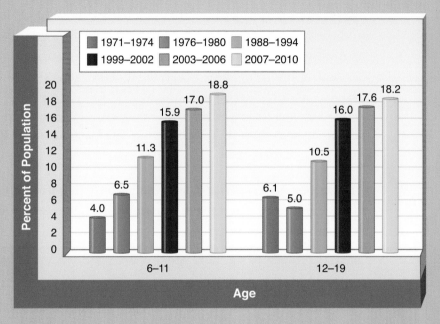

Taken from: NHANES: 1971–1974, 1976–1980, 1988–1994, 1999–2002, 2003–2006 and 2007–2010; Data derived from Health, United States, 2011 (NCHS). "Statistical Fact Sheet: 2013 Update: Overweight & Obesity." American Heart Association, 2013. www.heart.org/idc/groups/heart-public/@wcm/@sop/@smd/documents/downloadable /ucm_319588.pdf.

The first, obvious limitation of this study is that it examined mortality (death) but not morbidity (illness). The Global Burden of Disease Study, recently published in *The Lancet* [medical journal] and sponsored by the World Health Organization, the World Bank, and the Bill and Melinda Gates Foundation, is widely acknowledged as one of the most comprehensive epidemiologic assessments in history. What it shows, among countries around the world, is that we are living longer, but sicker. Thanks to the cutting edge of biomedical advance, we can often forestall death; but high-tech medicine is not remotely as useful for cultivating health and vitality.

Being Thin Is Not Necessarily Healthy

So, it's no surprise that overweight and mild obesity do not increase mortality. They could cause an enormous burden of chronic disease and still not [increase mortality].

But why would overweight and mild obesity be associated with a lower rate of mortality, as the meta-analysis suggests? For one thing, when people get sick, they generally lose weight. The new study was in no way adjusted to exclude from the analysis people who were thin because they were sick. We have long had evidence that among older people, hanging onto weight is associated with better outcomes than losing weight.

Second, in a society where a vast majority of the whole population is either overweight or obese, who isn't? Well, to some extent,

The author believes that a lean weight due to a healthful lifestyle and a lean weight due to anorexia nervosa or routine drug use are vastly different.

thin and healthy people. But also, along with those who have chronic disease, there are smokers (the meta-analysis only partly corrected for this), alcoholics, people with eating disorders, people who use illicit drugs, people with severe depression, and so on. There is an enormous difference between being lean because of eating well and being physically active, and being lean because of anorexia nervosa or routine cocaine use. The meta-analysis was blind to any such distinctions.

And, lastly . . . there is the fact that while overall obesity rates in the U.S. are showing signs of stabilizing, the rate of severe obesity—the very variety even this meta-analysis associates with a 30 percent or more increase in mortality risk—is "skyrocketing."

There are two implications of this. First, it is ever less useful to ask, "How many of us are overweight?" and ever more important to start asking, "How overweight are the many of us?" And second, since as a society we are getting ever heavier, it stands to reason that those who manage to remain only overweight are, in fact, doing something right—and deriving health benefits accordingly. The danger in using the new study to renounce concerns about weight, as Campos suggests, is that we invite weight gain—which will take us from overweight, to mildly obese, to more severely so. Those who are overweight but stably so aren't ignoring their health and weight; they are controlling them.

Obesity Is Strongly Associated with Chronic Disease

As for why those prepared to toss out everything we thought we knew about the health risks of obesity are not just wrong, but alarmingly so—let me count the reasons!

1. As noted, the Global Burden of Disease report indicates that mortality is not the real menace—it's morbidity. Obesity is consistently, powerfully associated with the risk of chronic disease.

2. When I was in medical school, we learned about "adult-onset" diabetes. That is now called "Type 2" diabetes because it occurs routinely in kids as well. It occurs routinely in kids because of epidemic childhood obesity.

3. The CDC [Centers for Disease Control and Prevention] is projecting that by mid-century, up to 1 in 3 Americans will be diabetic, due almost entirely to epidemic obesity. The trend is already well under way.

4. For those doubting, as Prof. Campos seems to, that obesity is the cause of all this diabetes and chronic disease, there is the Diabetes Prevention Program—which demonstrates that a 7 percent loss in body weight produces a 58 percent reduction in the development of diabetes among high-risk adults.

5. Studies spanning 20 years show a decisive association between healthful lifestyle practices, with resulting weight control, and a dramatic reduction in both chronic morbidity and premature mortality.

6. Unlike Prof. Campos, who is a lawyer, I am a doctor—I take care of patients, including those wrestling with weight control. Over 20 years, I have seen personally the changes in health and vitality when people who are obese become lean through the application of sensible and sustainable lifestyle practices.

7. My colleagues in pediatrics tell me routinely they are not only seeing Type 2 diabetes, but also fatty liver disease in overweight and obese children. When the obesity goes away, so do these ominous conditions.

8. A 35 percent increase in the rate of stroke has been reported among 5-to-14-year-olds in the U.S., and the only smoking gun on the scene to account for it is epidemic childhood obesity.

9. A study in roughly a million people that *did* control for chronic illness found a strong and consistent association between the body mass index and the risk of death, and cancer.

10. The BMI is known to be a crude measure that does not account for whether weight is muscle or fat, and if fat, where on the body it resides. The evidence that excess body fat particularly around the middle is harmful is indisputable.

The Epidemic of Obesity Is a
Clear and Present Danger

I guess, if Campos is right, this is all a myth. But since I actually see the evidence of it personally, as do many of my colleagues, it must be more than just a myth; it must be some kind of mass hallucination. Those, I think, are our choices. We are having a shared, population-level hallucination about the implications of epidemic obesity; or Prof. Campos is wrong. Choose.

Iconoclasts who see what the rest of the world overlooks are occasionally right. Copernicus and Galileo were right. Newton and Einstein were right. But the company is rarefied.

Most of the time, those who refute conventional wisdom profit from notoriety at our collective expense and are, in time, proven to be wrong. . . .

We can, of course, become unduly focused on body weight. In fact, as a culture we do so routinely. Weight is not the issue; health is the issue. It is possible to be heavier and healthy, or thinner and sick. We should keep our eyes on the prize. And the new meta-analysis may suggest that the range of "normal" for weight could be expanded, although it by no means proves it.

But at the population level, epidemic obesity is incontrovertibly established as a clear and all-but-omnipresent danger. It is absurd to suggest otherwise. And it's those who do so, who play ping-pong with science because of misguided bias or motivated self-interest—who threaten to forestall the societal action needed to turn this toxic tide—who frighten the hell out of me!

ELEVEN

A Woman Describes the Consequences of Dieting to Try to Be Like Her Naturally Thin Sister

Eva Believer

> Eva Believer is a pianist from Hendon, an area of northwest London. In the following selection Believer describes how being naturally overweight, in contrast to her naturally thin sister, affected her life. Extreme dieting in an attempt to emulate her sister's physique took a toll on her emotional and physical health, she reports. Eventually, she says, she learned to accept herself the way she is, and has become much happier and healthier as a result.

Standing alone on the other side of the bar, I watched my sister Egle flirt with a crowd of men and my whole body flinched with envy.

With her bodycon dress showing off her slender size-eight figure [a US size 4], men couldn't get enough of her. But who'd want her fat older sister, hiding in the corner?

As much as I loved my baby sister, I couldn't help but feel envious that she'd inherited 'skinny' genes. As we grew older, it was driving a wedge between us.

We had an age gap of just three years, and were close when we were young. Egle and I did everything together, from singing lessons to shopping. We'd always looked alike, too.

Adolescent Weight Gain

But when I hit my teens, I rapidly gained weight. Not wanting to be different from my sister, I carried on eating the same sized portions as she did, served up by my mum, Loreta, 55, a teacher.

By the time I was 18 and 5ft 7in, I tipped the scales at 13 ½ st [stone, or 185 pounds]. Secretly, I hoped Egle would follow my lead, but she could scoff a fried breakfast followed by cake and not put on a pound. She had an amazing figure with long legs and a tiny waist. It seemed so unfair.

I became jealous of the attention she got from men. I started to socialise with curvier friends instead, and would refuse to stand next to her in photos.

I had to get dresses custom-made, as shops didn't sell the latest trends in size 20 [US size 16]. By June 2002, my self-esteem was on the floor. Having completed my degree in performing arts at university, I ballooned to a size 24 [US size 20] and a whopping 17 ½ st [245 pounds] after comfort eating my way through exam revision.

I was constantly single and, seeing Egle date a string of men, decided my weight was holding me back. After a consultation at a health clinic, I started the blood group diet, where you eat specific foods dependent on your blood type.

Dieting "Success"

For my blood group, type A, breakfast was fruit instead of bacon and fried potatoes, pizza was traded for porridge at lunch, and fatty takeaways [takeout food] were replaced with fish and veg for dinner. I ate dangerously few calories a day, and invested in regular colonic irrigation treatments and lipo massages that promised to break down fat cells.

Within six months, my weight had dropped to 10 st [140 pounds]. I was working as a professional pianist and singer, and

I'M ON THE "LOW-FAT, LOW-CARB,
TURN-INTO-A-MOODY-GROUCH-AND-LOSE-
ALL-YOUR-FRIENDS" DIET.

© Everyday People Cartoons by Cathy Thorne.

could slip into size-12 evening gowns [US size 8] for concerts. On the outside I looked amazing. But did I feel it? Not one bit.

By June 2003, I was finally a size eight [US size 4] and just 8 ½ st [119 pounds]. I thought I'd be happy, but all I could see were my imperfections—like the tiny roll of flab that hung over the top of my jeans. I experienced mood swings and piercing headaches and constantly felt agitated and forgetful.

I was always hungry and food controlled my every thought. At night, I'd lie awake unable to sleep for the gnawing hunger and I'd eat slices of lemon in salt to suppress my appetite.

Reaching the Breaking Point

Friends and family who saw my weight loss were overjoyed for me. I couldn't bear to reveal how miserable I felt—especially to Egle. She assumed that I was happier thinner, because that's what I'd wanted for so long. But in fact, I felt like a failure.

That summer, I started dating Peter, 38, an actor I met at work. "You'd look better with a few extra pounds on you," he said on our second date. He didn't mean it as a compliment, but I took it as one as it proved I was skinny.

I thought losing weight would make me more confident in bed, but I didn't feel sexy. My boobs shrunk from a 38DD to a 32D and I had to wear a push-up bra to feel attractive. It's no surprise the relationship fizzled out after four months.

The next four years were a blur of dieting. My obsession with my weight overshadowed everything else. When I sang a solo at a big concert in 2004, I wore a beautiful snug-fitting gown, but felt so weak that my voice crumbled.

By March 2007, I'd reached rock bottom. I was constantly exhausted and emotional, and confided in Egle that dieting was destroying my life. She was shocked when I confessed I'd always felt in competition with her—and that this was spurring me on to stay slim.

Quitting the Diet

Egle was supportive. She said no diet was worth that much pain and that I was beautiful whatever my size. After our chat, I quit the diet. I wanted my life back.

I felt guilty for eating substantial meals again and, within months, had piled the pounds back on—but at last I felt like myself. I started socialising more and my musical performances improved.

In March 2008, Egle and I moved in together and we're closer now than ever. My weight has plateaued at 15st 7lb [207 pounds]. I try to eat healthily, but when I open the fridge and see Egle's chocolate cake, it takes all my willpower to resist.

The author says her obsession with weight loss and not eating led to poor health.

Of course, I still wish I was slimmer. Most size-18 women [US size 14] do. But I'd rather be larger than miserable. Last summer, I secured a modelling contract with Tesco's F+F clothing range, which goes up to a size 28 [US size 24]. I'm still single, but I've had more attention from men than ever before, because I'm more confident.

Part of me will always be envious of Egle but, ultimately, it's our differences that make us who we are. I've stopped comparing myself to her—and finally feel comfortable in my own skin.

Egle's Perspective

Egle says:

> As sisters, Eva and I have shared so many experiences together, and it was hard watching her struggle with her weight because I couldn't empathise and felt helpless. I'm lucky that I've always had a fast metabolism and haven't had to think about my size.
>
> When Eva lost weight, I was so happy for her. But I had no idea how miserable she was, or that she was starving herself to be the same size as me. When she eventually opened up, I couldn't help but feel guilty. I knew we'd grown apart, but had never understood why.
>
> Now I've got my sister back again, and I couldn't be happier. Eva used to think the gene pool wasn't fairly distributed, but the funny thing is, I've always been envious of her bubbly personality and pretty face. Size definitely isn't everything.

What You Should Know About Dieting

Facts About Dieting and Obesity

According to the Centers for Disease Control and Prevention (CDC), in 2009,

- 33 percent of US adults were overweight (body mass index [BMI] of 25–29.9), and
- 34 percent of US adults were obese (BMI 30 or greater).

The 2012 report *Weight in America: Obesity, Eating Disorders, and Other Health Risks*, compiling data from various sources, reported that

- in 2008 an estimated 170 million children around the world under the age of 18 years were considered overweight or obese;
- in 2005–2008 almost three times as many US children aged 6 to 11 were seriously overweight compared with children of that age in 1976–1980;
- in 2005–2008 more than three times as many children aged 12 to 19 were seriously overweight compared with those in 1976–1980;
- in 1988–1994 and 2005–2008 the prevalence of overweight increased from 7.2 percent to 10.7 percent for children aged 2 to 5 and from 11.3 percent to 17.4 percent for those 6 to 11 years of age;
- in 2010, 32 percent of all US children were obese or over-weight;
- in 2009, 15.8 percent of all students in the United States were overweight;

- 17.2 percent of 9th-grade students were overweight compared with 14.7 percent of 12th-grade students;
- the percentage of overweight female students was: 17.9 percent of 9th graders, 16.9 percent of 10th graders, 13.5 percent of 11th graders, and 15.1 percent of 12th graders;
- the percentage of male students who were overweight was: 15.3 percent of 9th graders, 13.8 percent of 10th graders, 14.5 percent of 11th graders, and 17.7 percent of 12th graders;
- 33.1 percent of teenage girls in high school and 22.7 percent of teenage boys thought of themselves as overweight;
- 44.4 percent of students indicated they were trying to lose weight;
- 59.3 percent of female high school students indicated they were trying to lose weight, compared with 30.5 percent of male students;
- 67.9 percent of adolescent girls and 55.7 percent of adolescent boys exercise to lose weight or maintain their current weight;
- 51.6 percent of female adolescents and 28.4 percent of male adolescents indicated that they had attempted to control or lose weight by choosing low-fat foods or counting calories;
- 14.5 percent of adolescent females and 6.9 percent of adolescent males reported not eating for at least twenty-four hours in an attempt to lose or control weight;
- 6.3 percent of female adolescents and 3.8 percent of male adolescents took dieting supplements without being advised to do so by a doctor;
- a child with one obese parent has a 50 percent probability of being obese; and
- a child with two obese parents has an 80 percent probability of being obese.

An October 2008 report in the journal *Obesity* reported that if current trends were to continue, by 2030
- 86.3 percent of US adults would be overweight;
- 51.1 percent would be obese;

- the prevalence of overweight children would almost double; and
- medical costs associated with overweight/obesity would increase to between $860.7 billion and $956.9 billion, amounting to 16–18 percent of all US health-care costs.

According to a fact sheet published by the American Heart Association in 2012, the current rates of overweight and obesity in US adolescents costs approximately $254 billion per year ($46 billion in medical costs and $208 billion in productivity lost to premature disease and death).

A 2012 article by dietitian Evelyn Tribole, drawing on a variety of sources, reports that
- a study of twins in Finland in which one dieted and the other did not found that those who dieted once were two to three times more likely to end up overweight, in comparison with their twin who never dieted;
- a 2006 study found that teenagers who diet are twice as likely to become overweight compared with those who do not diet (at the beginning of the five-year study the dieters and non-dieters weighed the same);
- University of California, Los Angeles (UCLA) researchers examining thirty-one long-term studies of dieting found that up to two-thirds of those dieting ultimately regained more weight than they lost; and
- a three-year study published in 2009 of almost two thousand teens reported that dieting was the most significant predictor of new eating disorders.

US Health Habits

The 2012 report *Weight in America: Obesity, Eating Disorders, and Other Health Risks*, compiling data from various sources, reports that
- less than 17 percent of US children got sufficient exercise in 2010;

- only about 20 percent of teenagers consume at least five servings of vegetables and fruit per day, and only 18 percent get at least one hour of physical activity per day;
- 24.9 percent of students in high school play video games or use computers for at least three hours per day whereas 32.8 percent watch TV for at least three hours per day;
- in the seven days before a 2009 survey, only 13.8 percent of students ate vegetables three or more times per day;
- 33.9 percent of students said they drank fruit juice or ate fruit at least twice per day; and
- only 22.3 percent reported eating vegetables or fruits at least five times per day.

According to Gallup polls in 2008 and 2009,
- 27 percent of Americans exercised at least thirty minutes a day at least five days per week in 2009;
- an additional 24 percent exercised a minimum of thirty minutes/day three–four days/week;
- 49 percent indicated that they exercised for thirty minutes or more less than three days/week.

According to the Yale University research project Food Advertising to Children and Teens,
- over $4.2 billion was spent by the fast-food industry on advertising in 2009;
- on average, a child aged 2 to 5 sees 2.8 television ads each day for fast food whereas children aged 6 to 11 see an average of 3.5/day, and those aged 12 to 17 see 4.7/day;
- preschoolers saw 21 percent more fast-food advertisements in 2009 than in 2003 whereas school-aged children saw 34 percent more such ads, and teenagers saw 39 percent more such ads;
- McDonald's uses Internet-based marketing with children as young as 2 years old;
- every month in 2009, McDonald's websites were visited by 365,000 children and 294,000 adolescents;

- 84 percent of parents say they take their children to a fast-food restaurant once a week or more;
- out of 3,039 possible combinations of children's meals offered at restaurants, only 12 met nutrition guidelines for preschoolers, and only 15 met nutrition guidelines for older kids;
- only 17 percent of regular menu items at restaurants could be considered healthy options;
- desserts and snacks offered at restaurants have up to fifteen hundred calories—five times the two-hundred- to three-hundred-calorie snacks the American Dietetic Association recommends for active teens;
- a typical restaurant has fifteen signs promoting particular menu items whereas only 4 percent of those promote healthy options.

A 2007 US Food and Drug Administration study of over a thousand people in the United States that asked what diets they had used in the previous thirty days found that
- 19 percent had been on a low-fat diet;
- 16 percent had been on a low-carbohydrate diet;
- 13 percent had been on a low-sodium diet;
- 11 percent had been on a low-calorie diet;
- 11 percent had been on a low-cholesterol diet;
- 15 percent had been on a low-sugar diet;
- 15 percent had been on a weight-loss diet;
- 55 percent had been on "none of these";
- 32 percent whose BMI was in the normal range indicated that they exercised at least five days/week;
- 28 percent of overweight respondents indicated that they exercised five days/week or more; and
- 20 percent of obese respondents said that they exercised at least five days/week.

According to marketing research organization the NPD Group, in 2013,
- 20 percent of US adults said they were dieting in 2012, compared with 31 percent in 1991;

- 23 percent of women reported dieting in 2012, compared with 34 percent in 1992;
- an estimated 34 million US adults were dieting during the holiday season;
- during the first two weeks of January, the number of people in the United States who are dieting increases by 47 percent, for a total of 50 million dieters;
- in 2012, 27 percent of US dieters stayed on their diet for more than a year, compared with 22 percent in 2004.

Opinions About Health and Dieting

According to the results of a 2012 survey by the International Food Information Council Foundation,

- 55 percent of the US population is attempting to lose weight;
- 55 percent of US men and 48 percent of US women find it easier to figure out their taxes than to figure out what they should be eating to promote health;
- 76 percent of respondents reported difficulty in knowing what nutrition advice to believe, due to the advice seeming to change so frequently.

According to a 2011 poll by the Pew Research Center for the People & the Press,

- 57 percent of respondents said they would like the government to contribute significantly to reducing obesity in children whereas 39 percent said the government should not do so;
- only 19 percent of the respondents, however, rated tackling obesity as a top policy priority for the federal government;
- 69 percent of respondents under thirty would like the government to combat childhood obesity, compared with 45 percent of those sixty-five and older;
- 74 percent of African Americans and 83 percent of Hispanics would like to see the government play a strong role in combating childhood obesity, compared with 49 percent of whites.

According to Gallup polls in 2007–2009,

- 62 percent of respondents in 2009 indicated that they were over their ideal weight;
- 27 percent were making serious efforts to lose weight;
- whereas the CDC reported that as of 2009 more than two-thirds of Americans were overweight or obese, only 36 percent of those polled in 2009 felt they were overweight while 58 percent felt their weight was about right, and 6 percent believed they were underweight;
- 83 percent of Americans surveyed in 2007 believed obesity was "very harmful" while an additional 15 percent felt it was "somewhat harmful";
- 67 percent of respondents reported that someone's being significantly overweight did not affect their opinion of that person;
- 29 percent reported that someone's being significantly overweight would negatively impact their opinion of that person;
- 80 percent of those polled thought that being overweight resulted from lifestyle choices;
- 8 percent believed it resulted from genetic factors; and
- 10 percent believed being overweight resulted from a combination of genetic factors and lifestyle choices.

A 2007 *Wall Street Journal*/Harris Interactive poll of 2,503 US adults found that

- 84 percent saw childhood obesity as a significant problem;
- 85 percent of parents with children younger than twelve felt that parents have the biggest impact when it comes to reducing obesity in children;
- 94 percent believed schools need to encourage regular exercise;
- 89 percent felt parents should limit the time their children spend watching TV, playing video games, or using computers, as well as prompting children to be more physically active;
- 88 percent wanted schools to make sure that healthy foods are available;

- 83 percent believed parents needed to be more mindful of what their children are eating;
- 78 percent believed food advertisements aimed at children contribute significantly to the problem of childhood obesity;
- 60 percent wanted to see government regulation of food advertising aimed at children;
- 91 percent approved of "using child-friendly characters to promote healthier foods like fruits and vegetables";
- 73 percent approved of "limiting advertising to children to healthier foods that are lower in calories, fat and/or sugar";
- 64 percent said it would help to stop "using popular characters from television shows and movies to market products to children."

According to the NPD Group, reporting in 2013, in 2012, 23 percent of people in the United States felt that those who are not overweight look significantly more attractive, down from 55 percent who felt that way in 1985.

What You Should Do About Dieting

Gather Information

The first step in grappling with any complex and controversial issue is to be informed about it. Gather as much information as you can from a variety of sources. The essays in this book are an excellent starting point, representing a variety of viewpoints and approaches to the topic. Your school or local library will be another source of useful information; look there for relevant books, magazines, and encyclopedia entries. The Bibliography and Organizations to Contact section of this book will give you other useful starting points in gathering additional information.

An enormous amount of information is available about dieting, including articles in popular magazines, books, and websites. Many scientific articles are available on all aspects of the topic. If the information in such articles is too dense or technical, check the abstract at the beginning of the article, which provides a clear summary of the researcher's conclusions. Internet search engines such as Google will be helpful to you in your search.

Identify the Issues Involved

Once you have gathered your information, review it methodically to discover the key issues involved. What theories do people have about the cause(s) of obesity and about how to best cultivate health and fitness? What different types of diets exist? How effective is dieting, in the short and long terms? What are the risks and side effects of dieting? How are dieting and eating disorders related? How has the "ideal" body shape changed over time and in different cultures? How do the media and fashion world influence people's views of dieting and weight loss?

In exploring this topic, it is worthwhile to examine the beliefs and practices of other cultures and time periods about health, diet, and body image. This will help provide a broader perspective on what is happening in America today and provide a deeper context for your own explorations.

Evaluate Your Sources

In developing your own opinion, it is vital to evaluate the sources of the information you have discovered. Authors of books, magazine articles, blogs etc., however well-intentioned, have their own perspectives and biases, which may affect how they perceive or present information on the subject. Dieting is a very complex and controversial topic, and much of the information available is of dubious quality. The dieting and weight-loss industries are worth many billions of dollars per year, and promoters of particular diets or weight-loss techniques may have a greater interest in their own financial well-being than in your health.

Consider the authors' credentials and what organizations they are affiliated with. For example, someone who heads a weight-loss clinic will likely present information that favors his or her particular technique of dieting, and may minimize or ignore data that suggest risks or side effects. Someone who is part of the "fat acceptance" or "body diversity" movements is likely to emphasize information and perspectives that call into question the utility or safety of any dieting technique and to minimize or ignore information about health dangers presented by being overweight and obese. Always critically evaluate and assess your sources rather than take whatever they say at face value.

Examine Your Own Perspective

Dieting, obesity, and body image are highly charged issues in modern society, especially for girls and women (though, increasingly, for boys and men as well). The media typically portray body ideals that are impossible for most people to attain. The messages you have received from family members, friends, and the media throughout your life will also affect your own thoughts and feelings on these topics. How do you feel about your body? Do you have a healthy relationship with food and exercise? How do your friends and family members relate to food and body issues?

If you are personally considering dieting, consider questions such as: Why do you want to lose weight? Is there obesity in your family (which would make it more challenging for you to lose weight)? Is there any family history of eating disorders, obsessive dieting, or mental illnesses such as obsessive-compulsive disorder? (If so, dieting could be particularly dangerous for you.) Is your primary goal to be healthy or to be a particular weight? Are you interested in dieting for yourself, or are you trying to lose weight for someone else, such as a girlfriend/boyfriend, parent, etc.? Lifestyle changes are more likely to be effective and appropriate when they are self-motivated, rather than done to please someone else.

In exploring any issue, be wary of "confirmation bias," the tendency to seek out information that confirms what one already believes to be true, and to discount information that contradicts preexisting beliefs. Deliberately counter this tendency by seeking out perspectives that contradict your current beliefs.

Form an Opinion and Take Action

Once you have gathered and organized information, identified the issues involved, and examined your own perspective, you will be ready to form an opinion on dieting and to advocate your position in debates and discussions. Perhaps you find yourself in agreement with one of the perspectives you have encountered on dieting, or perhaps you believe that several approaches working together are required to adequately address the issue. You might even decide that none of the perspectives you have encountered are convincing to you and that you cannot take a decisive position as yet. If that is the case, ask yourself what you would need to know to make up your mind; perhaps a bit more research would be helpful. Whatever position you take, be prepared to explain it clearly based on facts, evidence, and well-thought-out beliefs.

If you decide to try dieting yourself, make sure you have thoroughly researched the topic in general, as well as the particular diet you would like to experiment with. Make sure that you actually need to lose weight—a doctor or nutritionist will help you determine this. These professionals can also help you see that there is more to a healthy diet than just shedding pounds and that choosing the wrong diet for you can be harmful or even fatal. Positive long-term lifestyle choices are healthier, more sustainable, and safer than quick-weight-loss schemes. Remember that the ultimate goal is to be healthy, rather than to simply lose weight, and that it is very important to approach this in a safe and balanced way. Be sure to consult your family and your doctor and keep them in the loop.

The editors have compiled the following list of organizations concerned with the issues debated in this book. The descriptions are derived from materials provided by the organizations. All have publications or information available for interested readers. The list was compiled on the date of publication of the present volume; names, addresses, phone and fax numbers, and e-mail and Internet addresses may change. Be aware that many organizations take several weeks or longer to respond to inquiries, so allow as much time as possible.

Academy of Nutrition and Dietetics
120 S. Riverside Plaza, Ste. 2000
Chicago, IL 60606-6995
(800) 877-1600
e-mail: amacmunn@eatright.org
website: www.eatright.org

The Academy of Nutrition and Dietetics was originally founded as the American Dietetic Association in Cleveland, Ohio, in 1917, by a group of women dedicated to helping the government conserve food and improve the public's health and nutrition during World War I. It is the largest organization of food and nutrition professionals in the United States, working to shape the food choices and nutritional status of the public for optimal nutrition, health, and well-being. The association publishes the monthly *Journal of the Academy of Nutrition and Dietetics* (www.adajournal.org) as well as a variety of booklets, pamphlets, and fact sheets about nutrition.

**American Academy of Child and
Adolescent Psychiatry (AACAP)**
3615 Wisconsin Ave. NW
Washington, DC 20016
(202) 966-7300

fax: (202) 966-2891
e-mail: communications@aacap.org
website: www.aacap.org

AACAP is a nonprofit organization dedicated to providing parents and families with information regarding developmental, behavioral, and mental disorders that affect children and adolescents. The academy is composed of child and adolescent psychiatrists who actively research, evaluate, diagnose, and treat psychiatric disorders, including anorexia and bulimia, as well as related disorders. The organization provides information to the public through the distribution of the newsletter *Facts for Families* and the monthly *Journal of the American Academy of Child and Adolescent Psychiatry*.

American Heart Association (AHA)
7272 Greenville Ave.
Dallas, TX 75231
(800) 242-8721
website: www.heart.org

AHA is committed to fighting heart disease and stroke and to raising awareness of these diseases. As part of its mission, the association focuses on specific causes designed to help people achieve a heart-healthy lifestyle. Each of these cause initiatives reaches out to the public with resources and information to help people take positive action. The "Getting Healthy" section of AHA's website has a variety of information on nutrition and weight management. Entering the search term "dieting" in the search bar yields thousands of results.

American Psychological Association (APA)
750 First St. NE
Washington, DC 20002-4242
(202) 336-5500; toll-free: (800) 374-2721
e-mail: public.affairs@apa.org
website: www.apa.org

The APA is a scientific and professional organization representing psychology in the United States. With 150,000 members, the APA is the largest association of psychologists in the world. The APA website includes information on obesity, eating disorders, and related matters. Entering "dieting" in the search bar yields dozens of results.

American Society for Bariatric Surgery
100 SW Seventy-Fifth St., Ste. 201
Gainesville, FL 32607
(352) 331-4900
fax: (352) 331-4975
e-mail: info@asmbs.org
website: www.asbs.org

The purpose of the American Society for Bariatric Surgery is to advance the art and science of bariatric surgery by encouraging its members to pursue investigations in both the clinic and the laboratory; to exchange ideas, information, and experience pertaining to bariatric surgery; to promote guidelines for ethical patient selection and care; to develop educational programs for physicians, paramedical persons, and laypeople; and to promote outcome studies and quality assurance.

Anorexia Nervosa and Related Eating Disorders (ANRED)
PO Box 5102
Eugene, OR 97405
(541) 344-1144
e-mail: info@anred.com
website: www.anred.com

ANRED is a nonprofit organization that provides information about anorexia nervosa, bulimia nervosa, binge-eating disorder, compulsive exercising, and other lesser-known food and weight disorders, including details about recovery and prevention. ANRED offers workshops, individual and professional training, and local community education. It also produces a monthly newsletter.

Centers for Disease Control and Prevention (CDC)
1600 Clifton Rd. NE
Atlanta, GA 30333
(800) 232-4636
website: www.cdc.gov

The CDC strives to protect people's health and safety, to provide reliable health information, and to improve the health of Americans. The steps needed to accomplish this mission are based on scientific excellence, requiring well-trained public-health practitioners and leaders dedicated to high standards of quality and ethical practice. The organization's website contains a wealth of information related to dieting and health. Of particular interest is the Division of Nutrition, Physical Activity, and Obesity, which has sections on healthy weight, nutrition, physical activity, and overweight and obesity.

International Food Information Council Foundation (IFIC)
1100 Connecticut Ave. NW, Ste. 430
Washington, DC 20036
(202) 296-6540
e-mail: info@foodinsight.org
website: www.foodinsight.org

The IFIC is dedicated to the mission of effectively communicating science-based information on health, nutrition, and food safety for the public good. Its website serves as a nutrition and food safety resource for consumers, health professionals, journalists, educators, government officials, and students, providing resources on a variety of topics such as weight management, diet (food) and health, food safety, food production, and international food issues. The IFIC website features a blog and FoodInsightTV, which includes "Ask an Expert," "Person on the Street," webcasts, and educational videos. FoodInsightTV includes sections titled "weight management," and "diet (food) and health." IFIC also maintains a presence on Facebook, Twitter, and YouTube.

Mayo Clinic
13400 E. Shea Blvd.
Scottsdale, AZ 85259
(480) 301-8000
fax: (480) 301-9310
website: www.mayoclinic.org

The famed Mayo Clinic, with locations in Rochester, Minnesota; Jacksonville, Florida; and Scottsdale/Phoenix, Arizona is a not-for-profit medical center that diagnoses and treats complex medical problems in every specialty. The Mayo Clinic maintains a useful website for the public with hundreds of articles and entries on dieting and weight loss. Of particular interest is the website's sections titled "Obesity" and "Healthy Lifestyle" that include information on nutrition and healthy eating, fitness, and weight loss.

National Association to Advance Fat Acceptance (NAAFA)
PO Box 4662
Foster City, CA 94404-0662
(916) 558-6880
website: www.naafa.org

NAAFA works through public education and activism to end weight-based discrimination and to improve the quality of life for overweight people. The association provides information about the disadvantages of weight-loss treatments and publishes the bimonthly *NAAFA Newsletter*.

Rudd Center for Food Policy & Obesity
Yale University
PO Box 208369
New Haven, CT 06520-8369
(203) 432-6700
fax: (203) 432-9674
e-mail: andrea.wilson@yale.edu
website: www.yaleruddcenter.org

The Rudd Center for Food Policy & Obesity is a nonprofit research and public policy organization devoted to improving the world's diet, preventing obesity, and reducing weight stigma. The center serves as a research institution and clearinghouse for resources that add to the understanding of the complex forces affecting how people eat, the stigmatization of overweight and obese people, and how individuals and society can change. The Rudd Center offers the monthly e-mail newsletter *Health Digest*. Its website includes sections on "Food Marketing to Youth, " "Schools, Families & Communities," and "Weight Bias & Stigma."

US Food and Drug Administration (FDA)
10903 New Hampshire Ave.
Silver Spring, MD 20993
(888) 463-6332
e-mail: webmail@oc.fda.gov
website: www.fda.gov

The FDA is a public health agency, charged with protecting American consumers by enforcing the Federal Food, Drug, and Cosmetic Act and several related public health laws. To carry out this mandate of consumer protection, the FDA has investigators and inspectors covering the country's almost ninety-five-thousand FDA-regulated businesses. Its publications include government documents, reports, fact sheets, and press announcements. Entering "weight loss" in the FDA website's search bar yields hundreds of results, including important information about harmful or misleading weight-loss products.

BIBLIOGRAPHY

Books

Linda Bacon, *Health at Every Size: The Surprising Truth About Your Weight*. Dallas: BenBella, 2010.

Kim Brittingham, *Read My Hips: How I Learned to Love My Body, Ditch Dieting, and Live Large*. New York: Three Rivers, 2011.

Jorge Cruise, *The 3-Hour Diet for Teens: Lose Weight and Feel Great in Two Weeks!* New York: HarperCollins, 2007.

Peter Karainsky, *Culinary Intelligence: The Art of Eating Healthy (and Really Well)*. New York: Knopf, 2012.

David A. Kessler, *The End of Overeating: Taking Control of the Insatiable American Appetite*. Emmaus, PA: Rodale, 2009.

Lesley Kinzel, *Two Whole Cakes: How to Stop Dieting and Learn to Love Your Body*. New York: Feminist, 2012.

Gina Kolata, *Rethinking Thin: The New Science of Weight Loss—and the Myths and Realities of Dieting*. New York: Farrar, Straus, and Giroux, 2007.

Sam MacDonald, *The Urban Hermit: A Memoir*. New York: St. Martin's, 2008.

Peter Menzel and Faith Aluisio, *What I Eat: Around the World in 80 Diets*. Napa, CA: Material World, 2010.

Linda Ojeda, *Safe Dieting for Teens*. Alameda, CA: Hunter House, 2008.

Michael Pollan and Maira Kalman, *Food Rules: An Eater's Manual*. New York: Penguin, 2011.

Darya Pino Rose, *Foodist: Using Real Food and Real Science to Lose Weight Without Dieting*. New York: HarperOne, 2013.

Ellen L. Shanley and Colleen A. Thompson, *Fueling the Teen Machine: What It Takes to Make Good Choices for Yourself Every Day*. Palo Alto, CA: Bull, 2011.

Gary Taubes, *Why We Get Fat and What to Do About It*. New York: Knopf, 2011.

Evelyn Tribole and Elyse Resch, *Intuitive Eating: A Revolutionary Program That Works*. 3rd ed. New York: St. Martin's Griffin, 2012.

Brian Wansink, *Mindless Eating: Why We Eat More than We Think*. New York: Bantam, 2006.

Jennifer Young, *Balance Your Life, Balance the Scale: Ditch Dieting, Amp Up Your Energy, Feel Amazing, and Release the Weight*. New York: HarperOne, 2012.

Periodicals & Internet Sources

Stephanie Covington Armstrong, "When to Quit Dieting," *New York Times*, February 14, 2013.

Allison Aubrey, "Research: A Little Extra Fat May Help You Live Longer," *Morning Edition*, National Public Radio, January 2, 2013. www.npr.org/blogs/health/2013/01/02/168437030/research-a-little-extra-fat-may-help-you-live-longer.

Laura Beil, "Addicted to Food? The New Research Suggests It's Possible," *Daily Beast*, October 29, 2012. www.thedailybeast.com.

Mark Bittman, "Is Alzheimer's Type 3 Diabetes?," *Opinionator* (blog), *New York Times*, September 25, 2012. http://opinionator.blogs.nytimes.com.

Paul F. Campos, "Why the 'War on Fat' Is a Scam to Peddle Drugs," *Salon*, October 25, 2012. www.salon.com.

Richard Console, "Eating Cotton Balls? The Dark Side of Dieting," *Console & Hollawell Blog*, March 28, 2013. www.consoleandhollawell.com.

David Crary, "Skeptics Warn of Stigma amid 'War on Obesity,'" Association for Size Diversity and Health, May 1, 2011. www.sizediversityandhealth.org.

Melissa Dahl, "'The Drinking Man's Diet' and More Ways to Lose Weight in the 'Mad Men' Era," Health on *Today*, April 14, 2013. http://todayhealth.today.com.

The Economist, "Difference Engine: Food for Thought," May 19, 2012.

———, "Slim Pickings: Medical Treatments Are Unlikely to Reverse Obesity Rates in the Near Future," December 15, 2012.

Paula Goodyear, "Fixing Emotional Eating," Stuff, March 26, 2013. www.stuff.co.nz.

Gothamist, "Photo: 1912's Perfect Woman Was from Brooklyn, Weighed 171 Lbs, Had Pear-Shaped Body," December 20, 2012. http://gothamist.com.

Jayne Hurley and Bonnie Liebman, "Big: Movie Theaters Fill Buckets . . . and Bellies," *Nutrition Action Health Letter*, December 2009.

Marni Jameson, "A Reversal on Carbs: Fat Was Once the Devil. Now More Nutritionists Are Pointing Accusingly at Sugar and Refined Grains," *Los Angeles Times*, December 20, 2010.

Mandy Katz, "Tossing Out the Diet and Embracing the Fat," *New York Times*, July 15, 2009.

Lesley Kinzel, "Who's Really Surprised That 7-Year-Olds Are Putting Themselves on Diets?," XO Jane, March 13, 2013. www.xojane.com.

Gina Kolata, "Find Yourself Packing It On? Blame Friends," *New York Times*, July 26, 2007.

Jonah Lehrer, "A Chill Pill for Food's Thrill?," *Wall Street Journal*, March 3, 2012. http://online.wsj.com.

Meredith Melnick, "K–E Diet: Does It Work?," *Huffington Post*, April 18, 2012. www.huffingtonpost.com.

Marisa Meltzer, "The Fat Wars," *Daily Beast*, May 19, 2009. www.thedailybeast.com.

David Nakamura, "How Japan Defines 'Fat,'" *Atlantic Monthly*, November 10, 2009.

Tom Philpott, "Can Antibiotics Make You Fat?," *Mother Jones*, January 2, 2013.

Ronnie Polaneczky, "Dieting for Dollars," Philly.com, April 14, 2013. http://articles.philly.com.

Jen Quraishi, "The Twinkie Diet," *Mother Jones*, November 9, 2010.

Darya Pino Rose, "Foodist: Stop Dieting, Lose Weight," *Huffington Post*, May 6, 2013. www.huffingtonpost.com.

Peter Smith, "Watch Your Mouth: Eat Lightly and Carry a Big Fork. How Big Forks and Heavy Bowls Help You Eat Less," *Good*, August 8, 2011.

Kat Stoeffel, "Created by Men, Women Now Playing Public Diet Game," *New York*, April 25, 2013.

Margarita Tartakovsky, "Ditching Dieting: Celebrate International No Diet Day!," *Weightless with Margarita Tartakovsky* (blog), Psych Central, May 2013. http://blogs.psychcentral.com.

Teens Health, "The Deal with Diets," n.d. http://kidshealth.org.

Denise Winterman, "History's Weirdest Fad Diets," BBC News, January, 2013. www.bbc.co.uk.

INDEX

Wansink, Brian, 59

Weight
focus should be on health rather than, 35–36
heritability of, 17

Weight in America (Wexler), 5

Weight loss
dieting for, is completely ineffective, 16–24
is not necessary to be healthy, 34–39
percentage of US population attempting, 5, 7

The Weight of the Nation (documentary), 54–55, 58, 59, 62

WHO (World Health Organization), 71

Willpower, effective use of, 25–29

World Bank, 71

World Health Organization (WHO), 71

Y
Yo-yo dieting, 10, 13
is healthier than not dieting, 30–33

PICTURE CREDITS